∞

The Catholic Family Handbook

Other books
from Sophia Institute Press®
by the Reverend Lawrence G. Lovasik:

The Basic Book of Catholic Prayer

The Hidden Power of Kindness

The Catholic Family Handbook

Time-tested Techniques to Help You
Strengthen Your Marriage and Raise Good Kids

by the Reverend
Lawrence G. Lovasik

SOPHIA INSTITUTE PRESS®
Manchester, New Hampshire

The Catholic Family Handbook: Time-Tested Techniques to Help You Strengthen Your Marriage and Raise Good Kids is an abridged edition of Catholic Marriage and Child Care (Boston: The Christopher Publishing House, 1962) and contains editorial revisions to the original text.

Cover design: Coronation Media
in collaboration with Perceptions Design Studio.

On the cover: "Happy large family" (109391885)
© Gladskikh Tatiana / Shutterstock.com

Sophia Institute Press
Box 5284, Manchester, NH 03108
1-800-888-9344

www.SophiaInstitute.com
Sophia Institute Press® is a registered trademark of Sophia Institute.

Imprimi potest: Very Rev. Raymond J. Weisenberger, S.V.D.,
Provincial, Girard, Pennsylvania
Nihil obstat: Rt. Rev. Msgr. Wilfrid J. Nash, Litt.D., *Censor Librorum*
Imprimatur: John Mark Gannon, DD., D.C.L., LL.D.,
Archbishop of Erie

Library of Congress Cataloging-in-Publication Data

Lovasik, Lawrence G. (Lawrence George), 1913-
    The Catholic family handbook : time-tested techniques to help
you strengthen your marriage and raise good kids / by Lawrence G.
Lovasik. — Abridged ed.
        p. cm.
    Revised ed. of: Catholic marriage and child care. 1962.
    ISBN 1-928832-17-2 (pbk. : alk. paper)
    1. Family — Religious life. 2. Marriage — Religious aspects —
Catholic Church. 3. Catholic Church — Doctrines. I. Lovasik,
Lawrence G. (Lawrence George), 1913- Catholic marriage and child
care. II. Title.

    BX2351.L68 2000
    248.4'82 — dc21   00-057411

These chapters are
reverently dedicated to
the Holy Family of Nazareth —
Jesus, Mary, and Joseph —
the ideal of the Christian family

O Lord Jesus Christ,
who, by Your obedience to Mary and Joseph,
sanctified family life with splendid virtues,
grant that by their help, we may be instructed
by the example of Your Holy Family
and become partakers of their eternal happiness,
who live and reign forever. Amen.

∞

Contents

Part One
How to Strengthen Your Marriage

∞

Foreword

Dear husband and wife,

The purpose of these chapters on Catholic marriage and child care is to help restore marriage in Christ — to renew it according to the spirit of Christ — by offering Catholic couples simple but fundamental instruction on Catholic family life. Only if they live according to the principles given to us by Jesus Christ and His Church will they find true peace, love, and happiness in their family life.

The Catholic Church has constantly pointed out the way to success in marriage and happiness in family life. Her teachings have been tried and tested by time and eternity. I offer you here unfailing principles and sound advice, with the hope that they will help you to form your marriage according to the Christian ideal and your family according to the example of the Holy Family of Nazareth.

Father Lawrence G. Lovasik
Feast of the Holy Family
January 8, 1962
Divine Word Seminary

Editor's note: Except where otherwise noted, the biblical references in the following pages are based on the Revised Standard Version of the Old and New Testaments.

∞

The Catholic Family Handbook

Part One

∞

How to Strengthen Your Marriage

Chapter One

∞

Imitate the Holy Family

The life of the Holy Family at Nazareth was a hidden life of prayer and work. Their whole day's work was done for God alone, because prayer, simple and sublime, filled it completely. A charming simplicity dominated each of their domestic duties. Their disposition was always serene, because the thought of God absorbed them. Their hearts were in their home, and hence they could not be carried away on the stream of the world. They lived in retirement and poverty, being satisfied with only the necessities of life. Sanctity was so carefully concealed beneath the quiet simplicity of their daily life that people did not realize the Son of God and His Virgin Mother dwelt among them.

How reverently did Mary and Joseph admire the beautiful example of Jesus! What food for thought was His obedience! His practice of this difficult virtue gave to the hidden life of Nazareth its sweetness, peace, and majesty. Although He was the Son of God, He was subject to His parents — His creatures — for thirty years.

The example of His loving obedience should be an inspiration to children. They can expect the blessing of God — as

He promised in the Fourth Commandment[1] — if they respect and honor their parents.

We cannot measure the growth of Mary and Joseph in holiness. Grace poured constantly from Christ — its source — into their souls. While their hands were busy, Jesus absorbed their thoughts and affections and thrilled their hearts with the purest love for Him. Divine love united them all in a holy, happy family.

Our Lady is an attractive example for every wife and mother. Not only was she perfectly devoted to Joseph, her husband, but she was always an inspiration to him, especially in her love for her Son. It thrilled her with the purest joy to have so perfect a Model ever before her; to talk freely and often with Him; and to be so close an observer of His conduct. She filled her mind unceasingly with thoughts of His virtues. She pondered all His words and recorded them in her heart, as the Evangelist remarks.[2] She was absorbed in acquiring His spirit. She spent herself and was spent in learning the practical knowledge of Jesus Christ, and in so doing, she became the holiest creature who ever walked this earth.

Try to imitate this perfect dedication to God, and, like Mary, you will be most pleasing to Him and a source of inspiration and help to your family. Endeavor to burn with the same desire to imitate your Savior. The practical imitation of Christ is your highest duty. Mary can best teach you to imitate Him,

---

[1] "Honor your father and your mother, that your days may be long in the land which the Lord your God gives you" (Exod. 20:12).

[2] Luke 2:19.

because she is the Mirror of Justice, who reflects the spirit of Jesus most powerfully and most faithfully. Thus you will gain the knowledge that will aid you in bringing your family to eternal life.

As Mary, beautiful and perfect, is the sublime model for every Catholic wife, so Joseph, "the just man,"[3] gentle, kind, and chaste, is a model for every Catholic husband.

When God blesses your home with human life, the fruit of love, your family becomes like the Holy Family. In the family life of Jesus, Mary, and Joseph are exemplified the proper relations that should exist between husband and wife, parents and children. By practicing the domestic virtues of charity, obedience, and mutual help, Jesus, Mary, and Joseph sanctified family life.

∞

Model your home life on the holy house of Nazareth

The Holy Family lived in a plain cottage among other working people, in a village perched on a hillside. Although they did not enjoy modern conveniences, the three persons who lived there made it the happiest home that ever was. You cannot imagine any of them at any time thinking first of himself. This is the kind of home a husband likes to return to and to remain in. Mary saw to it that such was their home. She took it as her career to be a successful homemaker and mother.

And there was never a voice raised in that home. You cannot imagine Joseph shouting at his spouse and Mary screaming back at him, or the child Jesus answering impudently. You

[3] Matt. 1:19.

cannot imagine any of the three sulking or being moody and uncooperative.

In establishing your home, adopt the characteristics of the holy house of Nazareth. In proportion as you do so, you will have fashioned for yourselves a replica of the happiest home that ever was on earth.

The thought of the Holy Family suggests the love of simplicity. Domestic and marital happiness are closely bound up with the simple but good things of your state of life. Seek your happiness within the range of your income and your social, domestic, and family circles, and you will spare yourself many heartaches. Husband, be fair to your wife and family in trying to provide the necessities and ordinary comforts of life. Wife, strive to live within the income that is provided.

Be loyal to each other in periods of trial, and confidently seek the blessing of God at Mass, Holy Communion, and prayer. Pray often to the Holy Family to sanctify your family by their example and intercession, so that you may reach the ultimate goal of your marriage: the eternal possession of God.

In all your family needs and problems, confide in the intercession and help of Jesus, Mary, and Joseph. They will protect, guard, and keep you in holy fear, in peace, and in the harmony of Christian charity. By conforming yourselves to the divine model of this Holy Family, you will attain eternal happiness. Above all, through their prayers, you and your children will be enabled to honor God by a virtuous life so as to be worthy of a heavenly reward.

Every other consideration should yield to the thought of aiding each other to attain that goal. Only when religion permeates your daily life does your marriage fulfill its purpose. You and your children will find real happiness in direct proportion to your efforts to make God the very center of your married life. In this, the Holy Family should be your inspiration.

As a truly Catholic parent, try to copy the example of the Holy Family and to see in a hidden life of prayer, work, and daily fidelity to the commonplace, the surest steppingstone to sainthood.

As a family, try to lead a hidden life with Jesus in the Holy Eucharist. Through holy Mass, offer yourselves through Mary's hands as a sacrifice with Jesus; at Holy Communion, you will be changed into Jesus by divine grace so that you may live His life; by your visits to the tabernacle, you will enjoy His friendship in the midst of the many problems of life. If you have faith, you will discover His presence and see His veiled glory. If you love Him in the Holy Eucharist to the extent of making the Eucharist the center of your life, He will pour out His grace into your hearts and breathe the peace of God into your souls and make your burdens light. If you speak to Him, your God, with reverent familiarity, He will enlighten you about His Providence in your regard and strengthen you to bear the crosses He sends you. Devotion to the Holy Eucharist is the surest and easiest way of making your family resemble the Holy Family of Nazareth.

Joseph, the honest workman, is still the guardian of families. Mary, the Mother of God, is the blessed mother of every Catholic home. Jesus, subject to them — His creatures — is the model of every child. Through their intercession, may you and your family find your joy in God in this life, and may you be reunited to enjoy Him for all eternity in Heaven — as a family!

∞

Follow St. Paul's counsel

In his letter to the Ephesians, St. Paul gives us some general principles to follow in order to make family life truly Christian.

To the entire family, he says, "Always and for everything [give] thanks in the name of our Lord Jesus Christ to God the Father. Be subject to one another out of reverence for Christ."[4]

To wives he says, "Wives, be subject to your husbands, as to the Lord. For the husband is head of the wife as Christ is the head of the Church, His Body, and is Himself its Savior. As the Church is subject to Christ, so let wives also be subject in everything to their husbands."[5]

To husbands he says, "Husbands, love your wives, as Christ loved the Church and gave Himself up for her. . . . Even so husbands should love their wives as their own bodies. He who loves his wife loves himself."[6]

To children he says, "Children, obey your parents in the Lord, for this is right. 'Honor thy father and thy mother' (this is the first commandment with a promise), 'that it may be well with you and that you may live long on the earth.' "[7]

To fathers, he says, "Fathers, do not provoke your children to anger, but bring them up in the discipline and instruction of the Lord."[8]

---

[4] Eph. 5:20-21.
[5] Eph. 5:22-24.
[6] Eph. 5:25, 28.
[7] Eph. 6:1-3.
[8] Eph. 6:4.

This is the perfect solution to a major family problem. Let the wife be subject to her husband as if he were Christ. Let the husband love his wife as Christ loves the Church. If such a relationship existed between husband and wife, they would be in harmony as the Church and Christ are — in perfect love and peace. Finally, let children obey and respect their parents. If they do, God will bless them and grant peace to that family.

Chapter Two

∽

Reflect the dignity of God's fatherhood

Nature and Christian Tradition tell us that the father is the head of the home. That alone should suggest the dignity of fatherhood. Your dignity as a father rests, first of all, upon the fact that Almighty God has bestowed upon you the privilege of cooperating in the greatest natural mystery: the creation of human life. Sons and daughters are yours in a sense that nothing else you may ever possess can be called your own. That thought carries with it a unique honor. Even modern society, which has striven to forget the sanctity of marriage, retains this basic recognition.

Your children are your dependents. They bear your name. They imitate many of your mannerisms, gestures, and modes of thought. Much more: if you are a worthy father, and they are worthy children, they carry with them through life the training in virtue that you alone can impress on their young minds.

Pope Leo XIII[9] reminds each father that he is "the head of the family" and stresses that "the right of property which has been proved to belong to individual persons must also belong

---

[9] Leo XIII (1810-1903), Pope from 1878.

13

to the man as the head of the family." This follows logically, because "it is a most sacred law of nature that a father must provide food and all necessities for those whom he has begotten, as well as what is necessary to keep them from want and misery in the uncertainties of this mortal life. . . . The father's power is of such a nature that it cannot be destroyed or absorbed by the State, for it has the same origin as human life itself."

St. Thomas Aquinas[10] wrote, "The father according to the flesh has in a particular way a share in that principle which is in a manner universal found in God. . . . The father is the principle of generation, of education and discipline."

∽

Exert your fatherly authority early on
You should exert your authority as a father even when your children are babies. Your word should be something strong, good, and a little to be feared. If your children learn to respect your authority even from their tender years, they will find that authority a tremendous power to guide those difficult, almost uncontrollable years of adolescence. But if you let your wife do all the bossing, and are content to be another child yourself, you will be able to make only a feeble protest to youth's tendency to disobedience and independence.

It is never too soon for you to take up your position of authority as a father if you wish to have it established as a guide for your youngsters later on.

[10] St. Thomas Aquinas (c. 1225-1274), Dominican philosopher and theologian.

Reflect the dignity of God's fatherhood

Your children should enjoy the strength of your kind paternal authority. It gives them security. What is more, they are given security by the knowledge that their mother and father are united in matters of discipline. It is dangerous when a child can obtain from a softer parent something that he has failed to obtain from a stricter one, or when parents quarrel in front of children over points of conduct.

In the full program of domestic education, you must take great care that you use your authority properly. Pope Pius XI[11] said that normally a vocation to the priesthood is the result of the example and teaching of a father "strong in faith and manly in virtues."

Therefore, fatherhood is a vocation in God's service, to be held not lightly or frivolously, but with the serious determination of serious men. Since it is a life's work in His service, God offers His aid at every important step along the difficult road. On your part, though, He expects cooperation with grace, which in turn calls for persevering good will, a spirit of sacrifice, and conscientious observance of God's law made known by the Church.

---

[11] Pius XI (1857-1939), Pope from 1922.

Chapter Three

Guide your children
and shape their character

As the father is the head of the family, the mother is its heart. Just as Pope Pius XI speaks of the father as "strong in faith and manly in virtues," he speaks of a mother as "pure and devoted." Elsewhere he says, "As the father occupies the chief place in ruling, so the mother may and ought to claim for herself the chief place in love."

But the Holy Father speaks of supernatural love, not of the tender maternal love-instinct upon which the supernatural is built. Natural love, which is excellent in itself, and offers the possibility of untold good, may even at times be a hindrance when you are imprudent and cannot keep your children truly obedient, cannot refuse what is harmful, and cannot punish if necessary. It may be abused if it is made a wedge to separate the children from their father.

Supernatural love exercises the strongest appeal. Of it are born piety, modesty, purity, and fear of the Lord — all learned at the mother's knee.

Every person has a supernatural destiny, to be worked out in time. He must be educated for what he must be and what he must do here below, in order to attain the sublime end for which he was created. That education is the result of the combined efforts of both parents. But in his youngest years, the child is almost exclusively under the mother's guidance. Your efforts are to produce effects that will have their final reckoning in eternity.

Although your educational influence is of a nature entirely different from that of the father, your vocation as mother is equal in importance to your husband's. Most adults attest that mothers have had far more to do with the shaping of their character than fathers have. But so necessary are both that if either is lacking for any cause whatever, the education of the children is seriously, and sometimes fatally, handicapped.

As far as possible, be at home with your children. As you nourished your child before he was capable of eating solid food, so in the early formative years, nature has determined that you must nourish your child in virtue.

∽

Educate your children in spiritual matters

Some mothers do not seem to realize what a potential force for good they have at their fingertips. Some of them bemoan the fact that they are "just mothers" and shift their responsibility for the religious guardianship of their children entirely to the Church. This is a wrong attitude. You must live your Faith and, by example and direction, bear out the good points of the religious instruction your children receive at home or in school.

As a mother, you have a most rare chance of seeing into your children's hearts, if you will take the time to look. You are with your child in the mellow times of the day when troubled hearts most naturally open to a willing ear. In the matter of morals, boys as well as girls need help from their mothers. Teaching boys to respect holy purity carries added weight when the lesson is given by the very mothers they have loved and been taught to respect since infancy.

Instead of setting yourself up as a model of wisdom, it is much wiser for you to act the role of guide and confidante. This gives your child a much better feeling of security and fulfills your destiny of mother as well, because your children then find you a real individual in your own right. Personal success and happiness in life come only in the knowledge of our usefulness to others; as a mother, you have this opportunity in your own home at all times. You need not look elsewhere for it.

You cannot afford to be a part-time mother. You must have the courage and farsightedness to face all of your problems and must ask help from Him who is the source of all wisdom in the greatest and most worthy career a woman can espouse: being a real mother. The greatest joy you can find is in one day discovering that your daughters are as good as they are beautiful and your sons as pure as they are stalwart. When these youngsters are adolescents, you cannot let their minds and souls grow in just any haphazard fashion.

In a talk to women, Pope Pius XII[12] once said, "For this evil [languishing of faith and the fear of God, the infiltration of materialism], there is but one remedy: the strong faith for the parents, which, through example, religious instruction, and

[12] Pius XII (1876-1958), Pope from 1939.

moral education, will produce in children a solid faith . . . at the center of which there are the great religious truths.

"The example of parents — who does not know of its irreplaceable efficacy? The prayer of the father and the mother jointly with the children, the conscientious observance of the feasts, the respectful language when speaking of religion and the Church, the calmness, the diligence, honesty, loyalty and the irreprehensible conduct of life.

"Keep before the eyes of the child from his early years, the commandments of God and accustom him to observe them. . . . Counteract the desire for luxury and pleasure with an education in frankness and simplicity. Youth must learn again to control itself and face privation. . . . Educate youth in purity . . . in obedience and respect for authority."

As the educator and trainer of the immature minds and wills entrusted to you by God, your vocation is difficult. It calls for many qualities that are virtues in themselves: zeal, painstaking effort, patience in weariness, and the humility that joyfully stoops to the level of the child. It is hard work, and the temptation must come at times to abandon the effort and take life easy. Only the seriousness of the undertaking and the knowledge that it is done for God can sustain the untiring effort demanded.

On your wedding day, the priest prayed for the grace you need to carry out your duties as a mother: "May she be true and chaste . . . dear to her husband . . . wise . . . long-lived and faithful. . . . May she fortify her weakness with strong discipline . . . be grave in demeanor and honored for her modesty . . . well taught in heavenly love. . . . Let her life be good and sinless."

Guide your children and shape their character

The thought of the importance of your position as a Catholic mother should be a source of joy to you, but your battle will often be hard and your spiritual consolations few. It is good sometimes to know that although you have sacrificed many of the things modern "emancipated" women value so highly, your humble position is still the proudest in society. You are the possessor of the hand that rocks the cradle and rules the world. You are to be the comforter, the unchanging inspiration, and the educator of souls.

Chapter Four

∽

Make your home a place of harmony, goodness, and nobility

A good Catholic home is the one supreme need of the hour. And a good Catholic family life alone makes up a good Catholic home.

A good Catholic home is the source and maintainer of the Catholic way of life. We have many institutions that we call schools, but the real schools where the real lessons of life are learned are our homes. We hear a great deal about higher education, but the highest that can be had is found in the lofty lessons of self-control, self-sacrifice, sublime faith, and splendid trust, which home life has such a marvelous power to teach. There is no training to be had in school or college or anywhere in the world that can take the place of the discipline of the home. Even a public school from which every religious influence is banned cannot destroy the Catholic faith of children who come from wholesome Catholic homes.

It is difficult for a child to be better than his home environment or for a nation to be superior to the level of its home life. In fulfilling its double purpose — the generation and formation of children — the home becomes a little world in itself,

self-sufficient even in its youngest years. It is vital that you, as a mother or father, make of your home a training ground in character-building for your children, who will inherit the world's problems. Home is a place in which the young grow in harmony with all that is good and noble, where hardship, happiness, and work are shared.

Home should not be just a place. Rather, it must be *the* place. All else should be "outside." Home should be the center of activities and interests. It was built for births, courtship, marriage, and death. It is maintained so that children might grow, trained by precept and example — so that they will develop spiritually, mentally, and emotionally, just as they do physically.

Strong home ties have a tendency to weaken in children during high school. Then children work outside the home; they establish friendships independent of the family; they date; and they enjoy recreation away from the family. These are the years when family spirit is firmly cemented or broken, and the outcome depends, to a large extent, on youthful training. The more that parents and older brothers and sisters can do to focus all attention within the family, the better it is for the children.

To accomplish the high purpose set for its nature, and regulated by Divine Providence, the family must normally act as a unit. It is recognized as a unit by the Church, which cherishes and protects it as the basic unit of all society. The family should wield its influence and give a good example as a unit, particularly within its parish. This will be possible only if all the members have practiced the humbler virtues within the sanctuary of the home.

Make your home a place of harmony

As a Catholic parent, you must consecrate every intelligent effort to the task of developing the love of family as early as possible. Family consciousness, leading to intelligent love of family, is to be instilled from earliest childhood. There is need for a reasonable family pride. *Home, marriage, love,* and *children* are still the great heart-words of humanity and must continue to be so if civilization is not to sink.

∞

Let God build your home

The shortage of good homes is desperate. Why? It is just possible that we are not using the right Builder. The psalmist says, "Unless the Lord builds the house, those who build it labor in vain."[13]

When God builds, He starts with a solid four-square foundation: protection, discipline, education, and religion. As long as they remain the foundation, a house is a home. Without them, a house is no more than a hotel that offers quick meals, free beds, and bathroom facilities.

The Builder must live in the house He has built; otherwise, the foundations will crumble and the walls will come toppling down. If God is to protect and preserve your family, your family must welcome Him.

By going to Mass together, receiving Holy Communion as a family, and praying as a family, no longer are you two or five or seven individuals, but creatures and children of God, performing a single tremendous act of adoration, praise and thanksgiving, reparation, and petition, in union with Jesus

[13] Ps. 127:1.

Christ in His infinite Sacrifice in the Mass, which opens the floodgates of grace to you.

Then your home is a bulwark. Within its walls are love, understanding, and work for every member of the family with appropriate responsibilities and rewards. There you will find all the companionship and joy you can absorb, plenty of room for quiet and privacy when you want to be alone, time for talking, thinking, and enjoying the interchange of ideas, and, most important, time for growth in the things that matter — things that will lead you to God.

If the Lord builds your house, it is a home — God's. And that makes it Heaven on earth.

ᖌ

Protect the family as the foundation of society

The family is the foundation of society, the basic cell on which all the other agencies of society depend for the very existence and first formation of their members. A nation can flourish only to the extent that it is composed of mentally, morally, and physically healthy, thriving families.

From our homes will come the leaders of our country and of the world. A sound economic and social life and enduring world peace will be built from the materials our families supply. You must make every effort to develop the quality of your home life. If you cherish spiritual values, you will bind together domestic ties, for, as a parent, you play a leading part in rebuilding the ideals of a nation through its home and civic life. To a large degree, you form human character.

As a good parent, try to see all the problems of human life only in the perspective of the family. Your Christian sense of dignity should constantly put you on guard against any social or political order that threatens your mission as a parent, or the good of the family. Materialism endeavors to deprive family life of its very foundation of strength and happiness: faith in God and the principles of living taught by His divine Son.

Chapter Five

∽

Be open to the gift of children

Barring obstacles that God Himself may permit, ordinarily, when a couple marries, they should desire and gladly accept a large family.

Beware of false arguments against having a large family:

• *A large family costs too much.* You will agree if you love money above all things and you cannot stand to be deprived of any of the things that money buys for your neighbors. There are times when lack of money and indebtedness constitute a reason for using morally permissible means to delay having a child for a while. But money could hardly be put to better use than to pay for a doctor's care, delivery, and food and clothes for each new child.

• *Having many children wears a woman out before she reaches middle age.* Every good mother of a large family will agree that the inconvenience and pain connected with bearing and raising children are certainly not out of proportion to the joys and blessings of a large family. Many older mothers are a living proof that there is no truth to the statement that bearing many children wears a woman out before her time. Large families do not under usual circumstances destroy the health of mothers.

• *You cannot give all your children an expensive education when you have a large family.* The most important part of a child's education is received in the home and need not be expensive.

• *You cannot keep a neat, orderly home with many children.* But it is more important to have a truly happy home than a beautiful one.

If your large family brings ridicule from neighbors and even strangers, remember that you have a lasting treasure worth suffering for, and that the Lord called blessed those who suffer persecution for justice's sake. Those who ridicule may really be the ones who are doing something more vile than even animals would do, if they surrender their procreative powers to their love of money, comfort, and false pleasure.

Consider the advantages of having a large family:

• *You will be less exposed to the danger of sin.* If you fall prey to the obsession with limiting families to two or three children, which is common to many couples today, you may become a victim of the Devil's suggestions of artificial birth control.

Being busy with a large family is an excellent way of keeping out of sin, because temptations to be unfaithful are also greatly reduced. Small families make for much leisure, much social life, and many opportunities for

Be open to the gift of children

such temptations. Many an adultery and divorce could have been avoided if those involved had had large families.

• *You make the best possible use of life's most important years.* Instead of using the twenty to twenty-five years of mutual fertility — the average fertile time of the average marriage — in slaving to build up a business or making social conquests and indulging in selfish pleasures and comfort, you can do the best and greatest thing possible: work for God by bringing forth children whose souls are destined to be happy with God for all eternity.

• *The responsibilities of the family develop your God-given powers and help you to mature spiritually, mentally, and physically.* Spiritually, you become mature through surrender to God's will, through finding the particular role in which you can achieve your complete dedication to God. If you are wholly devoted to your task of bringing your family to God, you are a mature person whatever your age. A person who has never surrendered wholeheartedly to any purpose outside himself remains immature all his life.

In marriage you can develop a spirit of selflessness that makes your dedication deeper and richer with the years. Your service to your family expresses your love of God and increases your ability to love. You are unfolding those qualities of love, gentleness, and unselfish devotion that make you truly happy and truly great.

Mentally, you become mature in the various activities that you perform for those you love. In the family's day-to-day living, you can develop sound judgment and a keen insight into human nature. The responsibilities of your family life exercise your mental powers. Your intuition and powers of observation are called into play constantly to discover the unexpressed desires of your family, particularly the needs of small children. Your tact is valuable for the solution of the many problems of human relations and practical affairs that come up in the course of your day.

Physically, you become mature because marriage represents a development and completion for you. Childbearing gives new beauty and vitality to a woman, and fatherhood imparts stability and courage to a man.

• *You will offer the best atmosphere in which to develop character.* Nothing can take the place of day-to-day companionship with equals, under the wisely watchful and directing authority of good parents, to overcome selfishness, to build up charity, and to discipline all that is unruly in a person's nature. The child with only a single brother or sister, quite far removed in age, starts life under a handicap unknown to children of a large family.

Parents have a tendency to spoil their children by overindulging them or underdisciplining them. In a big family, it is necessary to spread one's love. Children are less subjected to selfishness and egotism.

In a large family there is not likely to be a spoiled child. The children themselves look to this. Since their parents may be hard-pressed to feed, clothe, house, and educate them, the children are urged to help them as much as they can. This encourages thrift, a valuable aid to success even in this world. Brothers and sisters have to get along with one another, and so the children in a large family learn teamwork, which is a splendid training for life.

• *You will be preparing the best material for vocations to the priesthood and the religious life.* Children are expected to make sacrifices for each other in a large family. From this spirit of sacrifice, a desire to sacrifice one's life can easily develop. Parents who practice birth control may be depriving the Church of many priests, brothers, and sisters who would help souls to reach Heaven.

Since older brothers and sisters often act as substitutes for their parents toward the younger children in many things, they learn, by experience, to fulfill the duties of motherhood and fatherhood. The wise, kind supervision of good parents enables them to become good parents themselves in their turn.

• *God will bless you especially in middle life and old age.* Grown children and grandchildren give parents of large families much joy and support. One of the saddest figures imaginable is a lonely father or mother who selfishly and sinfully limited his or her family to one or two children, especially if these children die or become delinquent.

Certainly you will experience heartaches and burdens, worries and difficulties, hard work and fatigue in the rearing of a large family. Nobody escapes these, because they are part of life and true accomplishment. But your accomplishment in rearing a large family will be glorious because your efforts will be so richly rewarded.

Children are often a trial and always a responsibility. The education of your children means that you must deprive yourself of luxuries and often of necessities, that you must give your time and leisure with unstinted devotion, and that you must cut down your legitimate opportunities for pleasure. Nothing that is precious or important is cheaply had or easily kept. The agony through which you passed as a mother, and the anxiety you experienced as a father, are in proportion to the importance of the souls you helped to bring into the world.

But since your children are so precious that Christ died for them and holds them in His arms, that God the Father adopted them as His own children at the baptismal font, that the Holy Spirit chose their bodies for His dwelling place, and that they will live as immortal citizens of God's kingdom, nothing is too much to expect — no sacrifice is too great to make for these astonishing objects of God's love.

When marriage and parenthood seem difficult, picture yourself with your spouse as an old couple who, just before you hear the Master's summoning call, look back along the road you have traveled. That road did not seem nearly so rough when you were leaning heavily upon each other. You faced threatening enemies on the way with stronger courage because you fought side by side. Courage sprang from knowing that you did not work or walk alone.

In spite of all its trials, your marriage promised you happiness in abundance. There was the first happiness of home-making and the supreme joy that came when you looked upon your firstborn and knew him to be yours. Strength came when you worked out life's problems together. You halved your sorrows and doubled your joys by sharing them. A noble pride thrilled you as your sons grew strong and your daughters charming.

Your heart was filled with joy as you led them closer to Christ in Holy Communion, or as you watched them receive the sacrament of Matrimony and begin their own families, or dedicate themselves to the service of God.

You will feel the calm happiness of turning your face toward Heaven with the sense of a gathered harvest. You can confidently expect to meet your Master waiting to bless you for a useful and holy life. Then you will really know that your life has been holier, happier, and more courageous because of the faithfully kept vows you took before the altar on the day of your wedding. With the calm confidence of those who have lived well and achieved nobly and left behind them the record of sanctified lives, you will pass into the presence of that Christ who was ever at your side with His grace — the first Guest at the wedding feast and the Lover of little children.

Chapter Six

∞

Do your part and trust in God's help

Happiness in marriage must be earned. It is something you must work out for yourself, chiefly by forgetting yourself and serving others. Marriage involves the art of human relations, the psychology of children, the economics of running a home, the maintenance of health, but, above all, the development of the moral and spiritual life of the family. All this demands a wide range of talents and skill. No marriage is a success unless you make it so, and that takes persistent effort and, still more, a constant and humble reliance on God.

The supreme object of your effort and striving is the family. You worked and saved in order that you might be married and have a home of your own. Once married, you worked and saved that you might successfully bring up a family. Your purpose in Matrimony should be to bring God's children into the world and rear them properly, to be one in body and spirit, and to make a happy home. You are to help one another and your children in every possible way, especially to get to Heaven, which is the final and eternal destiny for us all.

You and your spouse must be willing to work at marriage as the greatest job of your lives and not desert when problems arise. When you married, each of you took on a responsibility for some part of the work that goes into the making of a home. Both assume the responsibility of encouraging and helping the other, insofar as is possible, in the specific tasks designed for each. The training of children is the mutual responsibility of both husband and wife.

Thus, marriage is very much a fifty-fifty proposition. Only when you are willing to bear your share of the burdens of married life can you hope to have real love and peace.

Marriage is normally a source of equilibrium for you, because it brings you legitimate and healthy pleasures. But equilibrium always consists of an effort to impose the guidance of reason upon all your activities. Welcome without narrow-mindedness and weakness the joy marriage offers; use your reason in meeting the difficulties that marriage inevitably entails.

If your temperament is inherently unstable, if your life is weighed down with unfavorable conditions, you can recover the health of your emotional and spiritual life only if you seek above all what is right according to the sane reason that God has given you, providing, of course, that you make yourself do it. Only this effort can bring you the joy that is worthy of you.

∽

Avoid the tendency to be irresponsible

Love can be destroyed if you show no interest in and offer no help and encouragement for the work of your partner, or, what is worse, if you shirk and neglect your individual responsibilities to the family.

Irresponsibility is the failure to shoulder the basic obligations of marriage. An irresponsible husband considers himself entitled to all the privileges of marriage but frees himself from most of its responsibilities. Selfishness runs through such a person's entire makeup. Frequently he is waited on hand and foot and has never tried to think of others or to accept responsibility, with the result that he is emotionally immature, self-centered, and socially irresponsible.

Sometimes the wife is tied to her mother's apron strings and is emotionally immature. She refuses to shoulder the normal responsibility of a wife and mother.

Some married women harm their homes, their husbands, their children, and themselves by too much external activity: organizations, societies, luncheon groups, clubs, and civic committees. Birth control is a cause for too much social life. A childless or almost childless home can drive women to expend their God-given energies for motherhood on vain external affairs. Other causes are too much wealth and, therefore, too much leisure, so that even mothers of sizable families can hire people to do most of their work; and the appeal of social prominence.

Often fathers take little part in the administration of their homes and the raising of their families. Sometimes they use their jobs as a cloak for laziness in regard to their duties at home. They may be dynamos of energy in trying to make money and in getting ahead, but they refuse to help their wives or do anything for or with their children. Marriage is a partnership in which husband and wife are intended to work together for the decent upkeep of their home and, above all, the proper supervision and raising of children. Apart from his work at making a living, the husband is bound to help his wife at her tasks in any way that he can. To fail or refuse to do this is not only selfish, but also unfair. A husband may take an extra job to help his family financially or put in extra study to make himself fit for a better job, but he can do these things without completely neglecting his wife and children.

Then there is the husband who adopts the principle that, besides being faithful to his wife, the only contribution he is called upon to make toward the upkeep of a home and the raising of children is money. He selfishly imagines that it is his wife's part of the bargain to keep the home neat, to feed, clothe, and train the children, to correct and punish them — to do all the work involved in making a home and raising children by herself.

Such a husband proves himself to be lazy, inconsiderate, independent, and selfish. He may work eight hours a day in the office or shop, but his wife's work is never done and requires her to be on the go sixteen hours a day. He comes home from work and settles himself in front of the television or with the newspaper or behind closed doors and seldom raises a hand to help with the household chores or to keep the children occupied in a wholesome way. Saturdays, Sundays, and holidays are spent in the same way.

No matter what excuses may be made, this is an abuse and a cause of many of the failures in modern marriages. Irresponsibility is the third most frequent cause of broken marriages. Such irresponsible fathers should find a way to get around the excuses instead of permitting them to stand in the way of their active sharing in the important tasks of the home.

The wife of an irresponsible husband has a right to demand more consideration from him. If he fails to heed suggestions, a good wife can only take comfort from the family she is raising, and from the fact that the example of her patience may some-day make an impression upon her self-centered husband.

If a husband gambles away most of his time and money, it may be fundamentally because he has no incentive to find something better to do with them. A good wife must give him that incentive by making him want to be with her. She should do everything she can to make her home a place where her husband might desire to relax in peace or where he can be proud to bring his friends. She can make herself a pleasant hostess by entertaining his friends as well as her own. She can keep up her own external appearance, dress neatly and becom-ingly, and train her children to be good to their father when they are around him. Above all, she should never complain to her husband about the hard life she may lead.

Seeing his wife sacrificing her own tastes to his, a husband will be moved by sheer self-respect to sacrifice his tastes for her. Eventually he will realize that he has a fine, restful home, an intelligent wife, and children of whom he may be proud. He will appreciate such things and will want to show them off to his friends. A good wife will be compensated by the comfort that her orderly home and kind children will bring.

∽

Put your family ahead of your activities outside your home
Marriage demands companionship. The wish to be with the one loved is a sign of true love. To be satisfied being with each other only when this can hardly be avoided leads to tak-ing love for granted. Some husbands defend themselves by re-ferring to sins they do not commit, or to the money they bring in, or the work they do around the home.

Sometimes, as a father, you may feel more like spending your evenings at a club or at a meeting than at home with your wife and children; or, as a mother, you may feel more like engaging in activities outside your home than in making a true home for your husband and children. Your feelings must be subject both to your sense of duty and to the wishes of your partner and children.

So many people crowd their lives with too much activity and squeeze out of their schedule some of the things they would like to do or ought to do. They are doing many things that are good, but they are neglecting other things that are better and more important. Perhaps this is because they lose sight of the primacy of the obligations arising from their family and home.

Your first duty is to your home and family. You have solemnly sworn an obligation to work for their happiness and salvation. To be successful, families must be happy; and to be happy, the members must anticipate and fulfill the reasonable needs and desires of one another.

There is the husband who feels that he must have his nights out and his days off for bowling, golf, the club, the bar, and the gathering with the boys, but who rarely gives his wife an opportunity for relaxation away from the constant duties of the home. He considers it beneath his dignity to take his wife out with him once in a while. He might just as well say that she ought to enjoy staying home and working all the time, as if she were not a human being and, therefore, did not need recreation.

It is quite reasonable for a wife, whose life is confined almost entirely to the duties of the home, to long for some relaxation and change occasionally. A husband should be willing to make the sacrifice of some of the comfortable evenings at home so that he might offer his wife the opportunities for the relaxation she needs. He may have to cut down on some of his activities outside the home. If he gives a little more time to making his wife and children happy, he will find that he is getting a fair amount of relaxation and rest himself by sharing with them the simple joys of an occasional evening out together.

∞

Trust in God

You are assured of God's help. The Church teaches that through the sacrament of Matrimony, you and your spouse are assured of God's constant help. Therefore, you must firmly trust in God. In the next life, you may expect still greater blessings if on earth you have tried to build your home on the model of the Holy Family of Nazareth.

God is never outdone in generosity. If you serve Him as well as you can, you can be certain that He will bless you abundantly. If, on the other hand, you deliberately break His laws, you can be sure of depriving yourself and your family of His blessing.

The primary requisite for family happiness is union with God, who is the source of all happiness in this world and in the next. No one has such powerful means and more frequent opportunities of being united with God than a conscientious Catholic. Keep in touch with God through the frequent reception of the sacraments of Penance and the Eucharist and by much prayer.

Work hard for your family and their happiness as if every-thing depended upon you. Pray to God and trust Him even more, because everything really depends upon Him. Our Lord said, "Abide in me, and I in you. . . . Apart from me you can do nothing."[14]

[14] John 15:4, 5.

Chapter Seven

∞

Be patient

Patience is a powerful help in married life. It controls and re-strains angry feelings and outbursts of anger. It is a mature vir-tue that shows superiority of intellect, practical wisdom in daily life, strength of will, and a good, humble, and benevolent heart.

The more spiritual progress you make, the more patient and gentle you will become.

Patience procures for you love and influence. It attracts people to you and is of the utmost importance in the family, since you spend so much of your lives together.

Impatience, on the other hand, drives people away. It does no good and much harm, especially in the case of parents who are engaged in the rearing of children. Impatience is certainly not the spirit of Jesus.

In order to be patient, you must be prayerful and prepared for the inevitable unpleasantness in this life. Although you will never be able to arrange matters so that there will be nothing to provoke you to impatience, you can live by the principle that there is no reason in the world for getting impatient.

∞

Avoid being unjustly angry

Anger, which overrides the requirement of justice and charity, is a destroyer of family peace and happiness. There is such a thing as just anger, and even Christ became angry when He saw something wrong that deeply offended Him.[15] But anger is wrong when it is out of proportion to whatever occasioned it, when it becomes senseless fury, or when it accomplishes more harm than good.

In the family, you must practice forbearance, clemency, and patience, lest your children suffer from anger that runs wild. Anger is a homewrecker of deadly efficiency. It causes family members to lose respect for each other, and where respect is missing, love can hardly survive. If you indulge in anger frequently, conditions get worse instead of better, because you are constantly seeking new, sharper ways of hurting others. Anger leads to deep dislike and brooding hatred. This is the worst possible atmosphere in which to raise children.

Giving in to anger was condemned by Christ. Outbursts of temper are contrary to the whole idea of charity that He preached. There are occasions, however, when reasonable anger may be a forceful means of correction or the lesser of two evils. Scripture says, "Be angry, but sin not."[16] You may be justly angry when your spouse suggests something sinful. In that case, you are directing your anger to the correction or prevention of sin, and your anger may be justified if it is held in reasonable bounds. A short flurry of anger may at times be the

[15] Cf. Mark 3:1-5; John 2:14-16.
[16] Ps. 4:4.

lesser of two evils — for instance, if you are temperamentally inclined to hold a deep grudge for a long time unless you bring the matter into the open at the start and so end it.

A secretly nursed grudge may also be the cause of anger. A grudge is a permanent refusal to forgive a real or imaginary injury. As long as you hold a grudge, you are inviting anger, and you are in some degree responsible for anger in others. This anger can be detected in your tone of voice, in the silence of your mood, and in the very atmosphere of your home. If you want to prevent explosions of anger in your home, do not permit grudges to last more than a day.

Correction of temper is mostly a matter of self-control. Hide your feelings of displeasure. Be silent when you feel like saying harsh words. Cultivate a spirit of forgiveness and humility. You will seldom rejoice over your explosions of anger. But you will be glad that you did not say the things you wanted to say when you were angry.

∞

Be ready to compromise and to forgive

There will be many disagreements in your married life. Marriage has many difficulties and trials that are inevitable when two human beings live together in a life-long union of the greatest intimacy, with all the changes in mood and temperament that the varying conditions of life occasion. Self-sacrifice is one of the standards of measurement for true love. Self-sacrifice is opposed to selfishness. Selfishness means wanting your own way always. It makes you a dictator.

Self-sacrifice must take the form of compromise. This compromise does not surrender in matters of moral or spiritual principle, but does surrender in disputes over the use of money, leisure time, or material things. If you always insist on having your way, on doing what you want, on buying what you want, on going where you choose, without considering the desires of your partner, there is selfishness in place of love. Such self-ishness is the basis of all impatience, and anger is the fruit of impatience.

A happy marriage depends so much on cooperation, self-sacrifice, and understanding that whatever is gained by insisting on rights will be lost in peace and good will. So never talk about what you have a right to do against the wishes of your partner. It is difficult, if not impossible, to bring peace into a home where either the husband or the wife is stubbornly insisting on some right against the judgment or wishes of the partner.

You cannot force a person to be a good companion. That must come from the person's own desire and from his freedom from external tasks and worries. Rather than just laying down the law, you would do far better to show an interest in each other's work and to make some effort, even with all your own responsibilities, to help each other with it.

The partnership of marriage requires give and take. There are still husbands who feel that only men are entitled to free-dom of movement and outside-the-house contacts and associations. Either they are very jealous men, who unreasonably fear that they might lose their wives' affection if they permit them to mingle with people outside the home, or they are simply the dictator type, who feel that women should be subject to men and to their duties as wives and mothers, and that they should ask for nothing in the way of relaxation and recreation.

This is not normal, but it is something wives should accept patiently. They can use any reasonable means to correct the condition. Anger, resentment, and bitterness will not accomplish anything; rather they will serve only to harden some husbands in their unjust attitude.

If your husband has a kind of tyrannical temperament — if he thinks he knows it all as far as you are concerned — you will not change his opinion of his superior wisdom merely by butting your head against his will. You must have a full measure of respect for the judgment and wishes of your spouse. Use spiritual motives to accept with peace the tyranny you cannot avoid without war.

If your husband insists on making all the decisions, no matter how intimately you may be involved, then only by the grace of God, combined with a constant effort to cultivate patience, prudence, and tact will you be able to solve your problem. Furthermore, you accepted him "for better or for worse," and when "the worse" comes out in him, remember your promise at God's altar. Be thankful that you have a good Catholic husband, if that be the case, who does not, with all his faults, make it difficult for you to live up to your Faith and to save your soul.

∞

Be forgiving

Self-sacrifice must take the form of forgiveness. Forgiveness means the sacrifice of anger, bitterness, resentment, and revenge against your partner. There is no marriage in which forgiveness is not sometimes required, because there are no perfect human beings on earth. It is inevitable when you live with another person day after day that at times your feelings will be hurt, and you will think that your rights are abused. So do not be too sensitive, and do not feel sorry for yourself.

A nagging wife never wholeheartedly forgives, because she never lets her husband forget his faults and defects of character. A husband who bears grudges against his wife and enters into moody silences for long periods of time is too selfish to forgive from his heart.

The causes for disagreements are usually very trivial. If you have misunderstandings, do everything possible to straighten out these domestic problems as soon as possible, and try to keep harmony. Balance your accounts every day: if you quarrel in the morning, try to be at peace by nightfall. If you have failed, admit the mistake, and your spouse should forgive and forget.

You need a technique for handling the differences that so often lead to explosions of temper in marriage. Try to discuss your differences with calmness and understanding and settle them through reason tempered with good will and love. Without these elements, no disagreement can be solved. With the help of God and your good will, love, and understanding, a solution can be found for every difficulty.

Accept each other's faults. The state of being in love is not a sufficient guide to the new life of marriage, as a pagan, secular world would have us believe. The implications of the vows of Matrimony become clear only gradually.

When you were married, each of you had to choose first the interests of the other. This choice could not be accomplished in a matter of days. When you began to live as one, you discovered in yourselves faults of temper and character of which previously you may not have been aware. Even to this day you will find these faults your stumbling blocks. Your chance of happiness depends on your sincere determination and your capacity for self-sacrifice to get them out of your way.

Learn to accept each other's faults with patient love. Do not brood over them. If you do, you will pile one thing upon another and make mountains out of molehills. Forgiveness is especially a necessary part of your relationship. If you see a fault in your spouse that you consider serious, and which makes you unhappy, be patient and bring it up to your partner in a kind, prudent way.

Be ready to accept correction for your own faults and failings. If you have complaints about your spouse, begin the process of correction by examining and correcting yourself. A case cannot be settled on the basis of one spouse's complaints alone. The principal fault may be found on one side only, but you should not take it for granted without self-examination and humble self-improvement. You must dare to put aside your petty personal pattern, your peeves and fears, and in humble trust and prayer beg the help of God, offered to you in the sacrament of Matrimony.

Make unpleasant experiences fewer. There will be numerous occasions when even loving personalities verge on hatred. There will be spells of boredom and dreariness that even real love does not dispel. There will be days and nights of weariness, discouragement, unhappiness, and almost despair.

Remember that you have enough help to assure you of improvement. Both of you are working for the ideal marriage, and both of you are eager to find ways of making your life happier. If only you cooperate, God will give you innumerable graces — those particularly conferred by the sacrament of Matrimony — actual grace and sanctifying grace. This means a real lift to progress at the very moment you need it most.

∞

Ask God to help you be patient

Even people who constantly strive to please God have a goodly share of hard things to bear. This is the reason patience is so necessary for happiness in marriage. Be constantly prepared to bear disagreeable things. When there is an abundance of the good things, there is danger of becoming too occupied with passing and material considerations. Be grateful to God for them. When disagreeable things, reverses, sorrows, and disappointments come your way, put your confidence in God, who will strengthen you. Ask for patience. In the mercy of God, reverses are sometimes sent to awaken your wayward conscience or to test your love of God. When God so tests you, you must never be wanting in love and confidence and patience.

Chapter Eight

Be honest and sincere

You owe your spouse truth and sincerity. Our Lord is the greatest example of these virtues. He wished everyone well and was never anything but kindness itself in word and deed. He never made use of men for selfish ends, but spoke and acted openly, sincerely, and uprightly.

Honesty and sincerity bring about confidence and a spirit of loyalty. Few things contribute more to the success of a marriage. Such confidence bolsters a husband's flagging courage and inspires him with the will to win and to measure up to the high opinion that his wife and children have of him and his abilities.

The enemies of honesty and sincerity are nagging, miserliness, jealousy, and in-law trouble.

∞

Avoid nagging

Nagging is not always the fault of women, yet it seems that they often fall victims to this disagreeable habit that spoils family happiness. Do not be a nagging wife. Do not try to remake your husband. Prize your own individuality and be willing to put up with his. Do not expect your husband to render daily reports on where he was, why, when, and with whom. Be an eager listener, but a reluctant inquisitor.

You must assure yourself of your husband's unwavering devotion. The result of your placing implicit confidence and trust in him will not incline him to take advantage of your refusal to snoop or pry, or to step out of line. He will be won by decency, gratitude, loyalty, and trust, but never with fear.

A sincere and trusting wife will have a great influence in shaping her husband's life. Stand by your husband and share with head and heart his successes and failures. Give him due encouragement, but have the courage to drive home a sometimes unpleasant truth. Never be afraid of responsibility, but be prepared to embark on a new course of life with your husband, should the need arise. You will bring to your husband the love and inspiration he needs in the many problems of life, and that love and inspiration will weave threads of gold in his life's pattern.

Wealth, fame, and power are no satisfactory substitutes for the hard-earned joys of the married life, for not one of them can satisfy the hunger of the heart for love.

∞

Be temperate toward material things

Ill-regulated love of material things can be the cause of much trouble, unhappiness, and downright misery in the home. Your attitude toward money can be a source of great friction if it is not well ordered. Two extremes are to be avoided: miserliness and prodigality.

A miser lives in some comfort, but has to struggle mightily with himself to give away even a small sum. A spendthrift is one who foolishly, wastefully, and usually selfishly squanders money, whether he happens to possess little or much.

Today there is a craze for buying on credit. A wife who cannot see an expensive item for household use in a store without buying it can keep a man so loaded down with debt that he will find no joy in the use of these unpaid-for luxuries.

When a wife is foolish and childish in handling money, it would be prudent for a husband not to let her have any money at all. But such cases are rare.

The other extreme is intolerable miserliness. The principle is: "I pay as I go." Some men not only refuse to incur debts, but strive for a bank account ten times greater than the cost of anything their wives want to buy.

A little debt can be a good thing: it keeps both spouses striving and working together; whereas, without it, there is less incentive to cooperate and sacrifice. But that means a reasonable amount of debt. A sensible wife will accept limitations on her desire for new things, and at the same time a sensible husband will be willing to incur a reasonable debt.

Miserliness is not in accord with the honesty and sincerity you owe your family. If you are the father of a family, your first obligation is to provide the economic necessities for your wife and children. You are to be the breadwinner of the family, and you should not expect your wife to neglect your home and children for the sake of extra income unless extraordinary circumstances indicate a real need. A mother's job is to keep up a good home and raise her children properly. Greed or selfishness should not induce her to neglect these tasks for the sake of the additional income she can earn from a job outside the home.

In marriage you entered into the closest possible partnership with each other. The result of this partnership is that you are bound to share not only those faculties that are involved in the procreation of children, but other things as well, such as material possessions. The free use of material things is one of the greatest joys of ownership. If you, as a husband, deprive your wife of that joy, you are not sharing in the full sense of the word. The fact that you pay the bills does not mean that you are sharing these things completely.

Do not be a party to some of the abuses practiced by some "money-pinching" husbands. Do not keep from your wife the actual amount of your income or refuse to let her have a word to say about money matters, with the result that she has no idea how to buy for the present or to plan for the future. She has a right to know exactly how much you are earning, and she should be taken into your counsels on the economic planning for the home. Business dealings and other arrangements that affect the welfare of your home should be common knowledge. Neither of you should ever contract a personal debt without first talking it over with the other and reaching an agreement. A wise wife is satisfied with giving her honest opinion. The final decision rests with her husband, who is the head of the home, even as Christ is the head of the Church.

Do not imitate the practice of some husbands who give their wives just barely enough to provide necessities for the home, for herself, and for the children. Your wife should be a sharer of your income, not an unsalaried servant, held to account for every penny she spends.

Some husbands spend freely on their own amusements but cannot afford recreation money for their wives and children.

Your wife has a right to spend just as much of your money for her personal pleasure as you do for your own. The ideal arrangement is that both of you share in whatever pleasures money can buy.

∞

Combat your jealousy

Jealousy makes you eager to have all the affection and attention of your spouse. It may also be an enemy of honesty and sincerity, and consequently of love and harmony.

A jealous husband is one who feels uncertain about his wife's love — usually because he knows he is guilty of faults that make him undeserving of it — and who foolishly thinks that he can hold her loyalty to him only by preventing her from being friendly with anyone else. He deprives her of every kind of social life that he can forbid or prevent. He is suspicious of every innocent friendly contact his wife makes with others. He tries to keep her separated completely from her own family.

This jealous possessiveness transforms any feelings of love the wife once had for her husband into feelings of hate. It makes a wife's duty of fidelity to her husband much more difficult than it should be.

An unreasonably jealous wife is usually in some degree responsible for the wandering of her husband's love. It is natural that after several years of married life, some degree of taking one another for granted sets in. It would be better if the courtesy, consideration, and thoughtfulness that marked your courtship and the first years of marriage could survive through the years. Your husband may strain to appear his best before other women and show his worst side to you, not because he no longer loves you, but because he considers your love safely in his possession. This conduct is no reason for jealousy.

If you are a jealous wife, put yourself back into competition not only for your husband's love but also for his kindly attention. It is your job to win and hold, by giving proofs of your own love, the love you may think is turning away from you.

Jealousy is not a constant passion. Even if you have never felt the sting of jealousy, you may, under certain circumstances, experience a blind surge of it. Be resolved to avoid with utmost care those things which might awaken the passion of jealousy in your spouse.

∞

Be patient and understanding toward your in-laws

One of the most common sources of jealousy is in-law trouble, which can pull a couple apart more rapidly than many of the other disintegrating factors, if this is the chief reason for argument.

Marriage does not release a husband and wife from the duty of honoring and loving their mother and father. But it does make duties to their spouse supersede duties to their parents. That is what God said clearly of Adam, the first husband: "Therefore a man leaves his father and his mother and cleaves to his wife, and they become one flesh."[17]

Some husbands and wives never quite leave their mothers and fathers. They permit them to have more to say over their actions and plans than their spouses do.

[17] Gen. 2:24.

In-law trouble is very seldom caused solely by unreasonable jealousy on one side alone. If your spouse dislikes your relatives, look into yourself for whatever grounds you may have given for that aversion.

A wife who was spoiled and pampered by her family will sometimes seek an escape from new responsibility by running to those who will continue to baby her. At the first sign of disagreement, she will seek solace in the overindulgence of her parents. This will react unfavorably on her husband, who will gradually feel himself to be second in her affections when she has promised to hold him first. Thus, antagonism for the parents-in-law will grow with every incident.

If you are the husband of such a person, you will not awaken her to a sense of duty to you by violently asserting your rights or by using harsh language. Never look upon in-laws as rivals for your partner's affection. Filial love differs vastly from conjugal love, so there is room for both in the heart of every spouse. As in courtship, you won your wife from possible rivals by making yourself appear so kind and noble that she could not resist your appeal, so after marriage you have to prove yourself superior to her parents and relatives in devotion to her. You must back up your "rights" by continuous human expressions of love and interest. In this way, the competition between you and her relatives will soon end.

On the other hand, a husband who shows more than usual attachment to his parents almost always has trouble with jealousy on the part of his wife. He does not care what happens to his wife and children. His mother comes first. He takes her side against his wife. He lets his wife suffer rather than deal sternly with his mother. This is especially the case if he feels that even after marriage he must donate a large part of his income to his parents, even though they are not in great need.

Getting along with in-laws calls for tact and diplomacy. You must make allowance for the tendency of parents to think of their married son or daughter as their little child whom they wish to mother still. Try to keep the in-law relationships on an even keel by being patient and understanding, and you will have peace. If you think your husband is acting imprudently in giving help to his family, present your arguments to him in a kind way. You may even ask him to discuss the problem with a third and neutral person. Show goodwill by proposing a compromise.

Do not adopt a bitter, resentful attitude toward your husband, or say anything unkind about his relatives to him or to anyone else. Whether you win or lose your point, conquer and hide your feelings of bitterness. Showing them would be risking the peace and unity of your home. Security for the future is bought at too great a price if it means that you are to be divided in spirit by a deeply rooted grudge. Many a home has been wrecked by such resentment, and there is little comfort in the wreckage even if you maintain you were right.

∝

Give preference to your spouse

It is wise to establish distance from in-laws, if that is possible. It is true that there are many cases in which charity demands that an exception to this rule be made; nevertheless, there are other cases in which charity would be better served all around if some arrangement were made other than having an in-law in the same home.

After marriage, a wife's first duty is to her husband, not to her mother. If her mother remains with her, it should be only on the condition that she will say and do nothing that would in any way mar the relationship between husband and wife. If a mother who lives with her married daughter arouses suspicions in her daughter's mind, if she interferes with her right to run her own home, if she nags and complains and makes unreasonable demands, the best thing to do is to rent an apartment for her and let her live alone. Mothers-in-law should not be permitted to destroy family harmony.

When you can do nothing except offer your home to an in-law, at the very outset try to come to an understanding and agreement with all the parties concerned as to the conditions under which you will live in peace together. Let your in-law know that you are glad to be able to offer your home, but let it be made clear that the home remains yours, and that it is not to be spoiled by interference and meddling.

If there is no present way out of the difficulty, there may be room for an honest examination of conscience as to whether a wife is letting things get on her nerves that should be neutralized by a spirit of patience and charity. Small annoyances, unavoidable with two women in the same household, can be blown up into major irritations. God will give sufficient grace to bear these annoyances and to better the situation by prudent firmness and willing charity. The advice of a wise priestly confessor will help. A mother-in-law cannot be such a bad woman if she is the mother of the one you love very dearly.

It is most important that you show that you prefer your husband or wife to everyone else in the world. You refuse this sign of preference when you insist on living with a parent, or taking a parent into your home when there is no urgent reason of necessity or charity to do so. You are failing in your love if you pay more attention to what your parent wants than to what your spouse wants; if you are more concerned about your parent's welfare and happiness; if you let a parent rule the household; or if you take your parent's side in disputes. This is like going back on the promise you made in marriage and acting contrary to God's revealed plan for marriage.

Chapter Nine

∾

Practice kindness

Charity is practical love of our neighbor, the endeavor to do good to him in soul and body — mercy in the highest sense of the word. But love that resides in the soul ought to manifest itself through the body and its actions.

The Gospel says that Jesus "went about doing good,"[18] and in this He is a beautiful example for you. You have innumerable opportunities for doing good in your family. You have a heart, good thoughts, good words and deeds, and, above all, prayer. Kindness is never more important than in the family, and never more necessary than in parents.

∾

Be kind in thought

Without kind thoughts, there can be no real charity in the home. The thought eventually takes shape in words and works of charity, and gives to them their life, beauty, and worth. Words and works of charity are dead unless they are accompanied by a loving thought.

[18] Acts 10:38.

Kind thoughts preserve you from many sins against charity in your home. Uncharitable judgments, misunderstandings, suspicions, envy, jealousy, and uncharitable words will not take root in your soul if you think kind thoughts. Strained relations between your spouse or your children and you will be smoothed out, petty arguments will end of themselves, and aversions will disappear.

Kind thoughts are the secret of success in dealing with the members of your family. Only a kind person is able to judge another justly and make allowances for his weaknesses. As a mother or father, you wield the power to influence your children for good if your thoughts are always kind.

A kind thought never fails to bring joy to your home. It gladdens you and those around you. Happiness is not necessarily won by deeds, but it is readily held by a simple loving thought which can dispel the clouds of depression, discontent, and sadness. Your family will not fail to notice the presence of such thoughts, even if no word is spoken. If it should happen that no one is aware of the kind thought in your heart, God is aware of it, for He who Himself is Love knows all things.

You cooperate in God's work when you wish your spouse or your children well, when you implore God's blessing on their work and rejoice and thank God for their success. The good you do in this way will be rewarded more than any other because it is wholly selfless.

To foster kind thoughts, remember these suggestions:

• *Put yourself in the place of the other person*, and ask yourself how you would feel if you were the subject of such thoughts or judgments. Does God want this?

• *Remember your own faults.* Perhaps they are greater than those you condemn in others.

• *Remember the good points and virtues of others,* which usually outweigh their faults.

• *Try to find some excuse* for the things that others do which you do not like. This means having your eyes open to the whole truth, lest hasty judgments and prejudices close them to a part of the truth.

• *Forgive injuries* and try to make up at once with those who have offended you, or with those whom you have offended.

• *Be sympathetic.* Feel for others, and take a sincere interest in all that concerns them.

• *Try to see God in your spouse and children.* Love for your neighbor — and no one should be closer to you than your family — means loving God in your neighbor. This will lift your kindness to a supernatural plane and, at the same time, make it more generous, active, and universal.

• *Pray for your family* that God may be glorified in and through them. Above all, receive Holy Communion frequently, and ask Jesus to increase and preserve love in your heart for your family. If the Eucharist is the bond of charity that unites all Christians as members of one spiritual body, the Church, it is also the bond of charity that keeps your family together. By giving you a fuller share in the life of Christ, Holy Communion unites you more intimately to each other. It also gives you the help through actual grace to carry out God's great commandment of love in your own home, and to put away all unkindness. Through frequent Holy Communion, you will learn to overcome your selfishness and to resist your natural feelings of hatred and bitterness. You will develop kindness and sympathy, forbearance and forgiveness.

∞

Speak kindly

Kind words are a great blessing. They soothe, quiet, and comfort. When a kind word proceeds from your lips, it blesses you and fills others with gladness. If you greet your family with kind words and a cheerful disposition, even though you are at times weighed down by trials, you will put your worries to flight and lift your spirits.

As hatred breeds hatred, love creates love. There are many dispositions in people, but there is no one who will not respond to kindness and sympathy. Kind words have converted more sinners than zeal, eloquence, or learning.[19] Your spouse or children may sometimes betray bitterness toward you and expect unkindness. Respond with a word of kindness, and the rebellious one will be defenseless and often return the kindness. Each kind word will cost you only a moment in this world but will have an important bearing on how you will spend eternity.

[19] Cf. Frederick William Faber, *Spiritual Conferences* (Baltimore: John Murphy Company, 1859), 23.

∞

Avoid unkind words and the harm they do

• *Unkind words put others down.* By detraction, you make known the hidden faults of another without a good reason; by slander, you injure the good name of another by lying; and by harsh words of ridicule or contempt, you undermine the trust and confidence that should be the basis of family life.

• *Some of the worst sins in this matter are committed in the home by gossip.* Children hear their parents using abusive language to condemn their neighbors, to discuss their peculiarities, and to enlarge upon their shortcomings. It is a wicked thing to teach innocent children to become gossips. Gossip is all the more harmful when it has to do with a member of the family.

Do not listen to gossip about your spouse, much less be easily influenced by it. Gossip is often started by malicious informants who secretly hope to awaken jealousy. Mutual trust is a great aid toward the preservation of love and harmony in the home.

• *Harsh words more than harsh deeds are the termites that can undermine the foundation of a marriage.* Even though words seem like little things, so quickly and briefly spoken, do not minimize the power that lies in their bitterness. What you do is often easier to forgive than what you say.

Moreover, when an angry word provokes a quarrel, each party soon has a position to defend. A "principle" is at stake, you think, when in reality vanity and pride are the only principles involved. Reinforcements in the form of in-laws enter the picture; soon both sides are mobilized for an all-out war.

People will at least consider almost any suggestion made in a friendly manner. But they will bristle with resentment if it is shouted at them in ill temper. Not only words but even an angry tone can slam the door of understanding.

In disagreements, abusive words crowd the mouth, the doorway of the heart. Then stubbornness gets its chance, and the peace that a simple, kind word of apology could have quickly restored is rendered exceedingly difficult.

Too many marriages end up on the rocks because of little words and phrases. Many divorces could have been avoided if husband and wife had refrained from angry bickering and talked over their differences in a spirit of mutual understanding and goodwill.

Uncharitable talk should cause you deep concern, because it may be the source of great harm to your family. You have only to think of God's judgment and the account that you will have to render on your observance of the Eighth Commandment: "You shall not bear false witness against your neighbor."[20] If you thoughtlessly wag your tongue or make it the tool of anger or hatred; if you permit yourself to be swayed by bad temper, selfishness, and vanity; if you judge and blame rashly, try to begin to improve today for the love of God and your family.

[20] Exod. 20:16.

The following remedies may curb uncharitable talk in your family.

• *Learn to be silent*, especially when you are angry or disturbed, because silence is one of the great helps to avoid sin, to safeguard virtue, and to grow in close union with God. Do not repeat gossip and slander, even if by so doing you can hold the interest of your spouse, children, or friends. Carefully sift the talk you hear. Speak your mind, if you will, but mind what you speak.

• *Openly oppose uncharitable talk or counteract it by eloquent silence*. It is a great work of charity to show by your conduct that uncharitable talk disgusts you as much as impure stories do.

• *Have a sense of humor*, which comes to the rescue in many a trying situation. It enables you to see the funny side of a situation when your attention had been previously engrossed on the distressing side.

Do not save your sense of humor for parties; put it to work in your home, where it is needed most of all. The ability to see humor in a situation often enables you to extricate yourself from a predicament quickly. A good, hearty laugh will encourage a cheerful spirit in your family.

But good humor does not mean ridicule. A certain amount of good-humored kidding between husband and wife is usually a sign that they are getting along well. But if ridicule is used to sting and hurt, it is a sign that one has lost respect for the other.

• *Speak of events, not of people,* because a good name — that is, the esteem in which a person is held by his fellowmen and the mutual confidence resulting from this esteem — is a sacred thing, and everyone has a right to it. If you cannot say anything good about someone, say nothing at all.

• *Do not deceive yourself by false excuses for unkind talk,* such as, "It's not so bad or important," "What I said is true," or "I told him to keep it confidential." Consider the damage that might be done to a person's good name even in what you consider a trifling matter.

• *Avoid harsh and disrespectful words.* They wound the heart and disturb the soul. Wisecracks can hurt others, arouse resentment in them, and even engender hate. Avoid personal remarks and bitter sarcasm. If you wish to keep those you love close to you, laugh with them, not at them. You can destroy love by making scornful, sarcastic, belittling remarks to others, or by telling your friends jokes and humorous incidents that make a laughingstock of your spouse or your children.

At social gatherings, you can offend your spouse's and friends' sensibilities by displaying a form of rudeness that you would never tolerate from your children: How often do you interrupt a conversation to correct someone or to give your interpretation of what he is saying? How often do you contradict him?

• *Make a promise never to speak an angry word to your spouse.* Difficulties will arise between you and your

spouse, for you are only human. Yet there is no difficulty — no matter how serious — that cannot be settled if you talk it over in a calm, friendly manner.

If you are angry with your spouse, talk it out together.
You should share your grievances against each other in
loving sympathy: in this paradox lies a precious secret
to happiness. Psychiatrists testify that there is healing
in unbosoming ourselves to a sympathetic and friendly
listener. It restores peace of mind and a normal healthy
outlook. Troubles shared are troubles halved; troubles
hidden are troubles doubled.

True psychology is expressed in the Christian teaching that we must make peace with our adversary quickly,
by coming to an understanding with him.[21] What the
heart cries for is not an explosion but a release, and
the healthy way to achieve that release is for one person to make feelings of injury or injustice clear to the
other.

The words most difficult to say are: "I was at fault. . . .
I'm sorry. . . . Please forgive me." Yet the person who ut-
ters them first proves superiority in character and in
magnanimity and wins the greater victory.

Of course, it is destructive to swallow grudges and
nourish them quietly. You can rid yourself of resent-
ments without letting them boil up inside you. The best
way to approach such situations is to prevent them from
developing. If not nipped in the bud, the tendency to
quarrel can become chronic.

[21] Luke 12:58.

• *Be kind and considerate in speech.* Substitute expressions of kindness for quarreling and bitterness. Be quick to praise and commend, but slow to criticize. Take particular pains to see that you use your tongue for good, not for evil; to console, not to condemn; to build up, not to tear down; to rejoice at the good fortune of others, not to begrudge them success.

Reassure each other of your love in words of gratitude, appreciation, admiration, sympathy, comfort, and encouragement. Love needs and thrives on frequent assurances; it dwindles when it is rarely put into words.

• *Avoid idleness and gossip,* remembering our Lord's warning, "I tell you, on the day of judgment men will render account for every careless word they utter; for by your words you will be justified, and by your words you will be condemned."[22] As long as you devote yourself fully to your work, you will have neither the time nor the inclination to take part in unkind talk.

Above all, pray for each other. If you prayed for the members of your family half as much as you talk about their faults, how many sins would you avoid and how much happier your family life would be!

∞

Let your love show in kind deeds

Love is not content with words, but seeks to assert itself by deeds. The effect of love is an eagerness to give, to serve, and

[22] Matt. 12:36-37.

to console. If you do not wish to cease to love, you must never cease to do good.

Love in action calls for generosity and self-sacrifice. Without the element of self-sacrifice, you are pleasing only yourself. True charity makes the wants of your family your own. It makes you ready to anticipate the least of the needs or wishes of the members of your family and to render them all possible service. Sacrifices will bring joy if motivated by love.

* *Be glad to perform little services for each other.* Each day brings many opportunities for these unselfish actions. All the monotonous and unglamorous tasks — the duties of the day — will help you to find happiness if you perform them with unselfish love for each other, for your children, and for God. Love will move you to ease one another's burdens and to give help in time of need.

Even the little acts of politeness and courtesy, which are an accepted part of the relationship between men and women, can do much to make your home a pleasant place in which to live.

Courtesy is kindness manifested in your dealings with others. Intimacy should never destroy courtesy. You cannot possibly live in constant contact with others without noticing their faults and selfishness. Your own faults, like theirs, are bound to come to the surface. The observance of the courtesies of life — little acts of kindness and politeness — can smooth your relations with the members of your family and make them not only bearable, but, to a certain extent, pleasant.

Small signs of consideration for each other's ideas and plans are outward signs of interest, concern, and love for each other. Saying "Please," "Thank you," and "If you don't mind" will always have a pleasant effect. In the small things of daily living, you should treat each other with the same unfailing courtesy that you observe with strangers and friends.

Why should you sometimes be rude to each other just because you know that your family will understand? The closer you are to each other, the more gracious you ought to be.

• *Manifest your love by giving thoughtful gifts.* Love has sometimes been defined as the desire to give. Little outward gifts are but a reminder and expression of the gift of yourself and all you possess to your spouse. Such gifts need not be expensive or elaborate, but they should be marked by unexpectedness and understanding. Unexpectedness takes your gifts from the sphere of mere custom or routine, and understanding indicates a desire to bring special joy.

• *Give reasonable attention to your personal appearance.* This is a sign of respect and esteem. Even in the privacy of your home, make an effort to be clean and neatly dressed. This does not mean being dressed up at all times, as if you were entertaining company.

• *Let your charity be wholehearted and sympathetic,* for the manner of giving is worth more than the giving itself. Kindness is the art of pleasing, of contributing as much as possible to the ease and happiness of those with whom you associate. If you make it a point in your dealings with your family always to treat them as you would like to have them treat you, you will have no occasion for any breach of courtesy. Learn to think of others first.

If you wish to achieve an ideal marriage, one of the most important obligations you both have is to develop an attitude of loving consideration. This means a constant solicitude for the well-being of each other. Since you cannot exchange jobs, be interested in each other's work and activities, and try to understand the problems connected with them.

As a wife, you will become less inclined to talk about your own small irritations of the day if you try to understand what your husband's job involves, what demands are made upon him in a highly competitive world, and what he hopes to accomplish. This knowledge of what he faces each day in the outside world gives you greater incentive to make your home as clean, comfortable, and peaceful as you can. Make him always feel welcome, wanted, and the center of everything.

Most of all, try never to nag. Do not talk of failures, of the faults of his relatives, or of the mistakes of the past. There is nothing to be gained by renewed talk about annoying habits that he cannot or will not correct. You must endure them, and must not act like a martyr in doing so.

As a husband, you should have the same loving consideration for your wife. Try to understand what her job as a wife and mother involves, the demands it makes on her energy, time, and patience to keep your home in order and your children happy. It is good for you to remember her share in the burdens of caring for the children, doing household chores, cooking meals, dealing with money worries, addressing the problems of growing children, facing sickness, and meeting the demands of modern living. She will welcome a word of encouragement, but above all she will welcome understanding.

Gentleness, respect for the feelings of others, and consideration of their circumstances are the chief qualities of a gentleman or a lady. You have no better example to follow than that of Jesus and Mary.

• *Keep smiling* is a wonderful slogan for family life. A smile costs nothing but creates much. It enriches those who receive without impoverishing those who give. It creates happiness in the home and fosters good will. It is rest to the weary, daylight to the discouraged, sunshine to the sad, and nature's best antidote for trouble. Yet it cannot be bought, borrowed, or stolen, for it is something that is of no earthly good to anyone until it is given away.

The reward of kind deeds is very great. Kind deeds, like the love of God, have the power to make you truly holy. Love of your neighbor is but another form of the love of God. Kindness will make you a friend of Jesus, who said, "You are my friends if you do what I command you. . . . This is my commandment, that you love one another."[23]

---

[23] John 15:14, 12.

Practice kindness

Kind deeds are a source of happiness in the family. Little acts of kindness and little courtesies are the things that, added up at night, constitute a happy day. The best part of your life is spent in the little nameless acts of kindness and love you have performed in your home. Faithful, self-forgetting service — love that spends itself — is the secret of family happiness.

You will be judged and will gain merit in Heaven according to the spiritual and corporal works of mercy[24] you perform for the love of God. The blessing of God accompanies every kind deed. If our Lord promised that even a cup of cold water given in His name will not go without its reward,[25] He will grant you many graces and a heavenly reward for the services done to Him in the person of your wife or husband or child, whom He especially commands you to love.[26]

---

[24] The spiritual acts of mercy are to instruct the ignorant; to counsel the doubtful; to admonish sinners; to bear wrongs patiently; to forgive offenses willingly; to comfort the afflicted; and to pray for the living and the dead. The corporal acts of mercy are to feed the hungry; to give drink to the thirsty; to clothe the naked; to shelter the homeless; to visit the sick; to ransom the captive; and to bury the dead.

[25] Cf. Matt. 10:42.

[26] A comprehensive treatment of love of neighbor is found in my book *The Hidden Power of Kindness* (Manchester, New Hampshire: Sophia Institute Press, 1999).

Chapter Ten

∾

Strive for genuine love

The Church says that happiness comes as a by-product of duty
well done. It is earned, not found. The best way of achieving
conjugal happiness is by fulfilling the ends for which marriage
was instituted.

While the procreation of the race is the primary purpose of
marriage, there are other important ends achieved by this divine institution. Marriage fosters the love and devotion of
husband and wife. It provides a legitimate expression for the
divinely implanted sexual hunger. It answers man's craving for
intimate companionship, sympathy, understanding, and lasting friendship. It enriches the personality of man by increasing
his unselfishness and deepening his capacity for love, friendship, and sacrifice.

Although the physical elements of marriage are not to be
depreciated, the highest and most enduring joys are the mental and spiritual ones that come from the complete union of
hearts and souls — the perfect fusion of two personalities,
which is achieved only in the holy mystery of conjugal love.
The domestic affections — the mutual love of husband and
wife, of parents and children, of brothers and sisters — are the

principal source of human happiness and well-being, the chief wellsprings of actions, and also the chief safeguards against evil.

∞

Focus on the spiritual, not the physical

Love is not a mere emotion of the body. Merely emotional or sensual love is an attraction that arises within the body and concerns itself only with the body of another. To keep married persons from forgetting their primary duty to the race, God has implanted sexual hunger in human nature. It is part of the divine plan that the satisfaction of sexual hunger be accompanied by feelings of pleasure and happiness.

Emotional love eventually dies down after some years of marriage with the cooling of sentimental attraction. If a married person unfortunately comes to the point at which he can honestly say that his love for his spouse has completely died, this is usually an indication that it was only a selfish, sentimental, animal-like love from the very beginning.

Mere animal attraction may sometimes lead to marriage, but when it passes — as it always does — love passes, too, and usually some other animal attraction is sought and satisfied. Nothing is harder for a human being who possesses religious convictions and aspirations than to live long in marriage with a person who does practically nothing that a brute animal cannot do.

Therefore, in seeking happiness in marriage, do not stress what is physical. The fact is that only a small part of happiness in marriage is dependent upon the senses. Happiness and pleasure cannot be taken as a steady diet, because the Creator never meant people to be permanently happy here on earth. Physical attraction diminishes and gives place to a greater and nobler basis for happiness.

∽

Depend on your will, not on your feelings
The essence of love resides in the free will. The will may be stimulated to love freely by feelings and emotions. Love can be real and genuine without feelings if it is faithful and loyal, self-sacrificing and cooperative, and manifested in word and, more often, in deed. All this can be accomplished without a great deal of intense feeling.

All human love undergoes changes and varieties in feeling. This does not affect the motive of love residing in the will. The feelings of love ten years after marriage are not the same as they were on the day of marriage, and yet the love can be true and sincere. Duty is more important than feelings: loyalty to duty is fundamental in life; feelings are secondary and can, when the sense of duty is strong, be brought into satisfactory, if not perfect, agreement with the requirements of duty. If your sense of duty is uppermost in your mind, contrary feelings will never grow into hatred. Duties do not lose their force and obligation when opposed by contrary feelings; hence, a situation cannot become intolerable. People with some background of self-discipline seldom become victims of intolerable difficulties. It is important to check feelings that are contrary to duty from the very beginning, so they will never become strong.

Therefore, do not count too much on feelings of love as the only inspiration to fidelity throughout the years, but rely primarily on the conviction of obligation created by the vows you made in the marriage ceremony.

Nevertheless, feelings should not be neglected in your marriage, for it is possible to smother and destroy all the natural feelings of love. The sense of duty must always remain, but without any normal feeling, or with a feeling of revulsion instead of attraction, it will be difficult to live up to that sense of duty.

Since love is essentially an activity of the free will, once it is pledged in the marriage ceremony, it can and should, with the help of the grace of God, remain alive and strong forever. In that sense, it means working for the happiness of each other despite your own feelings and despite the faults and sins of your spouse. God uses the feelings of love, or a sense of emotional attraction between you, not only to lead you into marriage, but also to make carrying out the duties of marriage easier and more rewarding. You surely have one desire in marriage: to make the love that has drawn you together endure forever.

Love is destroyed only by a free act of the will. Your love for your spouse dies only if you really want it to die. Even then your love can be revived by doing the things necessary to promote love.

Love is not dead even if strong feelings are absent. Women generally remain romantic long after their wedding; men usually do not. Most women would like their husbands to be as obviously affectionate after ten or fifteen years of marriage as they were during courtship.

The best attitude to adopt toward the idea that your spouse does not love you is to look at it as a petty annoyance and try to dismiss it as one would dismiss an unwanted temptation. Add to that a determination to keep busy, preferably in some form of service to others, especially to your family. Permit yourself as little time to brood and worry as you possibly can. Idleness and introspection are dangerous. You can overcome this danger if you intensify your spiritual life by such practices as daily Mass and Communion, frequent prayers, visits to the Blessed Sacrament, and the cultivation of a childlike confidence in God's Providence and goodness.

If you begin to think that life is destroying the love you once had for your husband, you must rekindle the spark if you can. If a true love ever existed, it can be restored and increased. Your union is a permanent one, and you must not allow it, for want of love, to head toward estrangement and separation. You can recapture even a lost love by daily tending and constant watching for little opportunities to show your love. Your love will grow as your eager efforts increase.

Genuine love is a rational attraction, mutually shared, between two persons, that is not contrary to God's law or to one's own good of soul or body. It is a special inclination to do good for another, spiritually or physically, and to share all good with that person. Such love is rational, because it must be under the influence of the mind and will, which together direct it to what is not contrary to God's will or to the good of the person loving as well as of the person loved.

Love is not simply a blissful state that you fall into; it is an unselfish virtue that lifts you out of yourself. It is, above all, the desire to give — body, mind, and heart — to each other without reserve. Unless you are willing to give yourself completely, unless the first emphasis is on giving rather than on getting, you are not truly in love. Love is the desire that you and your spouse have to spend the rest of your lives together and to work out your salvation together. The principal reason for unhappiness in marriage is the failure to love.

Love is one of the noblest passions implanted by God in human nature. St. Thomas says that "to love is to will that good should befall a person."[27] Your love is genuine if it has God for its foundation; then it is an aid to reaching God. Love is a thing of the spirit more than of the flesh. When love shows itself only in the flesh, it may be more lust than love.

Religion alone brings out the full attractiveness of a human being. It alone provides the motives, actions, and practical precepts for the practice of the virtues that appeal most strongly to the love of another. Religion makes human beings higher and nobler than brute animals.

Genuine love will patch up differences and make marriage happy, provided religious motivation, self-sacrifice, prayer, and work are given their proper place in your life. Genuine love is enough for a happy marriage.

Love is not one-sided, but reciprocal. The love between husband and wife is the root from which grows perfect love between father, mother, and child. You must love each other before you can love your children perfectly.

⌘

Recognize and strive for the qualities of genuine love
If your love for each other is to be genuine, it must be unselfish, affectionate, practical, and exclusive.

[27] Cf. *Summa Theologica*, II-II, Q. 23, art. 1.

Genuine love is unselfish. Your love is selfish when you love your spouse for what he or she can give you by way of pleasure, convenience, or material advantages. Selfish love is one of the main reasons many marriages are unhappy and break up.

Your love is unselfish when you love your spouse for his or her sake, for what you can give. This unselfish love between human beings, when mutual, is called friendship. The most intimate and enduring friendship of all should be that between husband and wife. Among Christians, this love should be raised to the higher plane of supernatural charity — the love of another person because of the person's relationship to God.

When you chose each other for life, you did so because you loved each other and wished to give each other your entire self. Time will make its mark upon your physical attractions, but the gift of your mind and heart should grow with the years. The essence of marriage is this mutual outpouring of love, of your giving everything to each other.

The marriage bond has its likeness in the bond between Christ and the Church — namely, the bond of intense, strong love. Marital love is thus something quite distinct from lust. Lust seeks its own animal gratification, regardless of any other end but its own indulgence. Love, however, seeks the higher well-being. It will be selfless to such a degree that the weaker partner has every consideration. Whatever sensual pleasure may be incidental to this love, all will be controlled and directed to the higher well-being of husband, wife, and children.

The test of true unselfish love is the willingness to make sacrifices for the other. Marriage is give-and-take. Where there are two people, with different backgrounds and interests, conflicts of interest are inevitable. These points of conflict can be gracefully resolved only by unselfish love and the willingness to make sacrifices for one another. Our Lord tells us, "Greater love has no man than this, that a man lay down his life for his friends."[28] Love is proved by sacrifice. In many a married life, there is a need of this supreme test of human love.

By far, the greatest amount of human love and unselfishness in this world is found within the circle of family relationships. Family life calls for innumerable daily compromises and sacrifices. It calls for the shouldering of responsibilities and hardships for the good of the whole group. And if that sacrifice of self for the common good of others is done out of love for God, then indeed we have the fulfillment of the great Christian law of love. Then indeed the members of the family are well on their way to working out their salvation.

Such a family will at the same time be the highest credit to society, a most solid foundation for the nation. The more Christian the homes of a people are, the more Christian will be their society.

For a wife, an expression of sacrifice is obedience to her husband. When you and your spouse were joined in Matrimony, neither of you was perfect. Your mutual life and the constant adjustment of mind and heart, under the influence of matrimonial grace, are to make you perfect. Marriage is one of the means of your salvation.

The words of St. Paul indicate how the grace acts: "Wives, be subject to your husbands, as to the Lord. For the husband is head of the wife as Christ is the head of the Church. . . . As the Church is subject to Christ, so let wives also be subject in

[28] John 15:13.

everything to their husbands."[29] The apostle calls Matrimony a great sacrament and expresses the ideal of Catholic marriage. He sets up the proper relationship between husband and wife by indicating that the wife is to be obedient to the husband in things that are lawful.

This obedience does not mean a servile subjection, for the apostle goes on to say, "Husbands, love your wives, as Christ loved the Church and gave Himself up for her."[30] With such love binding her husband, a wife cannot resent her position.

The husband is the head of the house, but he should not be an unreasonable head. The wife is not a mere servant to the man, nor is she to be considered a minor. Pope Pius XI, in his Letter on Marriage,[31] said, "If the man is the head of the family, the woman is the heart, and as he occupies the chief place in ruling, so she may and ought to claim for herself the chief place in love."

No obedience is due to your husband when he is obviously demanding something contrary to divine law. You must refuse to obey when you are asked to commit an act that is against any of the Ten Commandments. In all cases of doubt, however, the presumption is in favor of the husband.

The exchange of the obedience of the wife for the love of the husband is a fair one. As a wife, you could not begrudge your obedience in lawful things when you know that for that obedience you are to be loved even as the Church is loved by Christ.

[29] Eph. 5:22-24.
[30] Eph. 5:25.
[31] December 31, 1930.

Above all, however, the obedience must have its foundation in mutual love. Unless there is present that determination to love each other through thick and thin, through success and through adversity, it will be useless to try to decide by argument who has the right to command and who the duty to obey.

As a wife, it is your duty to recognize this headship of your husband. You must place your husband first with yourself, first before the children, and first before your friends. You would hardly be living this out if, forgetting that you left mother and father for him, you constantly quoted your father's or your mother's opinions and what they would do under like circumstances, and if you flew to your mother with criticisms of your husband when things were not running smoothly. If your husband is truly first with you, you will not go to your parents with problems and complaints, but to your husband, on whom you must lean for advice and encouragement and understanding.

Even if your husband is not naturally assertive and not likely to take the lead and leaves many decisions and burdens to you, you can at least ask for his ideas and seek his counsel in the presence of your children.

With your husband absent from home for the major part of the day, you have more to do with the children than he has. Be especially careful to place him first in your conversation, and make opportunities for him to do things with the children when he is home.

A necessary means to unselfish love is knowing yourself — your own temperament, your own weakness, your own selfish leanings. For instance, if you are inclined by your temperament to moodiness and know that this is one of your weak points, you ought to wage a constant battle against it. If you do not recognize it as a weakness, you will give in to it constantly and make life miserable for your spouse. If you are inclined to domineer over others, unless you are conscious of this and strive against it, you will be constantly bossing your family.

The following points will help you to examine your conscience as to whether your love is selfish or unselfish.

As a husband, you have selfish love if:

• you look at your wife only as an attractive object who can satisfy your passion, keep your house in order, and prepare your food when you want it;

• you look upon yourself as the master of the house and want everything arranged for your convenience and pleasure, without a thought for your wife;

• you break out in ungovernable anger when your wishes are thwarted;

• you let your desire for pleasure and drink destroy your home and family;

• you never take your wife out for an evening of relaxation, but expect her to be no more than a servant;

• you think that because you make the money, it all belongs to you, and you spend it on yourself as you see fit, giving your wife only what is necessary for household expenses, as though you were doing her a favor;

• you do not even give your wife an idea of the state of your family's finances;

• you never give your wife any expression of affection, none of the signs of love of which a woman's heart has so much need;

• you are brutal, demanding, and without any consideration for your wife in the exercise of your marital rights.

As a wife, you have selfish love if:

• you see in your husband only a man who can provide you with security and material advantages;

• you complain or sulk when you do not get what you want;

• you feign illness to make it impossible for you to do your work and to gain sympathy and attention from others;

• you leave your house in disorder and neglect your children and your husband;

• you deny your husband the reasonable exercise of the marital rights that you contracted to give at the time of your marriage;

• you become bitter when you see that you are not becoming wealthy or influential;

• you are filled with jealousy, which gives way to irritability, bickering, and quarreling and drives all peace and joy from your home.

Since selfishness is so much a part of our fallen nature, it will demand constant effort to face up to your shortcomings and to try to conquer them. But only such effort will enable you to live at peace with yourself and others.

Genuine love is affectionate. Just because you pledged your love to your spouse in the marriage ceremony, it cannot thereafter be taken for granted. Love cannot and will not be taken for granted as residing in the soul, but it must be manifested habitually in external signs or actions. Human beings, made up of body and soul, need such expressions of love. It is the same in the practice of religion. The body must help the soul in expressing love toward God.

The husband who never gives any outward sign, by word or action, of the love he has for his wife does not have an affectionate love. If she were to ask him whether he still loves her, he would admit in an offhand way that he does. Such a statement does not mean a thing to his wife. The husband who refuses to manifest his love for his wife is usually the same one who refuses to lift a hand to help her with her domestic tasks. Apart from the sexual part of marriage, he wants to live his own self-centered, egotistic, independent life, as though he had never solemnly promised to enter into a wholehearted partnership with her in establishing a home.

If this love is to flourish, it must be fed. The need must be satisfied, or it will shrivel up. To cultivate such affection requires an active will and a keen intelligence. You should consider the cultivation of love an obligation in your married life. The great and emotional love of your wedding day will seem shallow compared with the deep, moving love of maturity — the love you have made grow.

As a husband, do not allow yourself to be moved merely by your passions and feelings, but use your intelligence to find out what little acts of sympathy, kindness, interest, and attention affect your wife's feelings toward you. Make a practice of frequently repeating such acts. No matter what you say, you do not truly love your wife unless you show and express that love in many day-to-day ways. Without the slightest insincerity, but with a renunciation of selfishness, you should often praise her appearance and her work; remember anniversaries with presents; express sympathy for her burdens; above all, just reassure her of your love.

It is important for both of you to learn the secret of cultivating affection, of making use of suffering only as an occasion for deeper sympathy, of studying each other's likes and dislikes, of saying the word that gives pleasure, and of avoiding the word that causes pain. If your love is genuine, it will be affectionate.

Genuine love is understanding and sympathetic. Selfishness is at the root of practically every given cause for divorce. The period of adaptation in marriage is critical. It calls for self-sacrificing and unselfish effort on the part of both of you to adjust yourselves to each other.

Understanding love is especially important in the use of sex in marriage. Unreasonableness in regard to sex is strictly a by-product of paganism and selfishness. The husband who considers sexual enjoyment as something he refuses to dispense with or moderate in any way does not have an understanding love. He believes that he has a right to as much of it as he desires. He may even demand it of his wife under any circumstances. The bad husband refuses to consider such circumstances as his wife's ill health, mental or physical; her many burdens with children; and his obligation to make the union between husband and wife a source of real joy and happiness to both.

If circumstances deprive him of what he selfishly considers his right, he refuses to seek the help God offers him in frequent Communion, and sometimes seeks sinful indulgences that make him a traitor to his wife and to God. Besides being selfish, unreasonable, and overly demanding of his wife, he may fail seriously by insisting that his wife cooperate with him in sins of contraception. This is the last stage in vileness, when a man uses his authority as head of the family to plunge both himself and his wife into continuing habits of sin that make both miserable.

If there is little of the self-sacrifice of Christ in the way you treat each other, there will be little of the compassionate love of Christ in your hearts. This calls for an intelligent attempt to understand your spouse, to appreciate his viewpoints in all things, to be considerate of his likes and dislikes, to compassionate his weakness, and to support his burdens. Without this consideration and adjustment, genuine love is impossible.

Marital happiness is won by understanding and sympathetic love. The going on the long road of marriage will not always be easy. If you want a successful marriage, you must learn the art of making your interest, understanding, sympathy, and appreciation penetrate your mutual strivings, hopes, fears, longings, and experiences. One of the principal joys of married life is found in the consciousness of mutual aid, comfort, and encouragement offered by a loyal helpmate walking at one's side. Love that is enriched with sympathy and understanding engenders loyalty, a solicitude for the happiness of the other, and an eagerness to serve. If you have attained a deep and understanding love, you share the company and comradeship of one another even when both of you are silent.

The grace of the sacrament of Matrimony does not mean that Christian marriages are always happy marriages, or even that the marriages of well-matched persons infallibly have happy endings. One thing, however, should console every Christian: the fact that, in the words of St. Paul, "to them that love God, all things work together unto good."[32]

Even failures can be sanctifying. Still, the fact that God often brings forth good from evil does not do away with your responsibility if you have done wrong. Even if your sanctification happens to begin when you realize that your husband is growing cool toward you, the misfortune that sanctifies you is nonetheless your husband's serious responsibility, if he is at fault. If you happen to be the cause of your husband's loss of affection, you also bear responsibility for the sin, although its consequences may be spiritually beneficial to him. Even when God makes such wonderful use of evil for your benefit, evil remains evil, and those who commit it bear the responsibility for it.

There are happy marriages only when husbands and wives love each other. And it is always possible to love. Even suffering, when it is borne together, can strengthen union and nurture your deepest and truest happiness.

Thus your feelings will mingle, and you will achieve a maximum of sharing, as the old proverb says, "Joys shared are doubled; sorrows shared are halved." In this way, mutual sympathy and understanding multiply the joys and lessen the sorrows of your married life.

[32] Rom. 8:28 (Douay-Rheims translation).

Genuine love is practical. Do not let any external attractions interfere with the attraction of your spouse. Do not be so absorbed in your work or business or profession as to regard your family and home as a secondary element in your life. Do not let the counterattraction of other pleasures — company, the club, or outside activity — crowd out your attraction for each other. All are transgressions on the practical love you owe each other.

A wife can tolerate such things only if she gets the affection to which she is entitled, because by nature she herself has such strong affection. A prolonged neglect of the practical side of your love may wear out your wife's affection, and that is the beginning of the end of all love and results in serious harm to family life. A practical love of your wife, that is, your paying attention to her appearance, her housekeeping, her health, and her pleasures, has consequences that are far-reaching. If your love is not expressed in action, you will fail in one of the greatest duties of your manhood.

An external sign of affection for a woman is to dress to please her husband. As a wife, you might greet your husband's return from work with a smiling face and neat attire. If your husband has a favorite color, wear it often. Improving your own appearance may be just as important as the time and effort you spend on the appearance of your home and your children.

As the years go by and children and duties become more pressing, try not to omit the small signs of love that show a warm and pleasant awareness of each other, such as a kiss hello or goodbye, a light caress or an understanding look, a word of praise and appreciation, help with the dishes or a repair job, an offer to mind the children, or an invitation to eat out.

You should not stop doing all the nice things you used to do during courtship or in the first days of your marriage. Birthday cakes, surprises, boxes of candy, and little presents are but so many efforts to ensure the freshness of the love of your wedding day.

Genuine love must be exclusive. The love of husband and wife must be exclusive. Avoid even innocent attentions to others that may possibly give displeasure to your spouse. Make special efforts to make your husband or wife realize that he or she is the only one who has any real attraction for you. If you cultivate this habit of thought and action, the mutual love between you will become so strong and constant as to leave no room for jealousy. Such love is strong as death.[33]

∽

Rely on God's grace

A wife and husband should love each other with a love that is unselfish, affectionate, sympathetic, practical, and exclusive. Neither of you can afford to leave these qualities to natural impulse. You must cultivate them and seek opportunities of expressing them in your daily life together. Only then will your love for each other be genuine, and only then will your marriage be truly happy.

All your obligations toward each other can be summed up in one sentence: "Love each other with all of your mind, heart, and body." This attitude of love will make your marriage soul-satisfying and spiritually rewarding. Turn toward each other with love, instead of inward in self-pity or selfishness.

[33] Cf. Song of Sol. 8:6.

Do not think in terms of obligations or duty, something you have to do. Even if you know that your spouse is giving only a grudging twenty percent of affection and effort, it should not matter. Your love and the help of grace will carry you to God.

If Jesus Christ is the object and desire of your strivings in the married state, if each of you attempts to be Christlike in your thoughts, desires, and actions, if Christ is not only the Unseen Guest, but the Enthroned King of your home, your marriage will be a happy one. God is Love, and all true human love is but a faint trickle from that Infinite Source. If you want to love or to be loved, go to the reservoir that knows no emptying: the Heart of Jesus Christ, the Son of God!

Part Two

∞

How to Raise Good Kids

∞

Chapter Eleven

Know your duties as a parent

Christian parenthood is sacred. Jesus Christ saw fit to exalt the human contract of man and woman, among the baptized, to the dignity of a sacrament. Christian marriage is a sacrament of the New Law to give grace to husband and wife so that they may rightly fulfill their duties toward one another and toward their children.

When in Holy Matrimony you cooperate with God in human creation, the union of your bodies, hearts, and souls is a symbol of the union and love of Christ and His spouse, the Church.

This fact should send you to your knees with a prayer for mutual sanctification — the first end of the sacrament — as well as the strong grace to carry out perfectly the duties of the high state of life to which God has called you in holy wedlock.

If you live in this spirit, you will look on every child as a precious gift from Heaven, a temple of the Holy Spirit, a future citizen of Heaven, and a living testimonial of your faith in and love for each other.

The rights of children may be summarized thus:

• To belong to a legitimate and indissoluble family;

• To enjoy a sound, balanced, and constructive family environment;

• To have opportunities for an economically worthy life;

• To have an education aimed at developing their faculties and training them as worthy members of society;

• To receive the means they need to develop their own vocation;

• To live in a wholesome social environment in which their personalities are respected;

• To be protected in the development of their physical strength;

• To enjoy sound recreation so as to channel their vitality;

• To be given kind and intelligent correction and guidance in the event of misbehavior;

• To have their spiritual potentialities fully cultivated as children of God.

Your duties toward your children are threefold:

• *Toward their bodies:* Take proper care of the health of your children, providing for them sufficient food, clothing, recreation, and medical attention.

• *Toward their minds:* Send your children to a Catholic school, or at least provide for their religious instruction. Help them to choose a vocation or profession, and help prepare them for it.

• *Toward their souls:* Guard your children against sin, aid them in the practice of virtue, counsel them in their problems, instruct them, and, above all, pray for them.

∞

Be unselfish as a parent

Parenthood demands generosity to assume, not only the honors and joys of motherhood and fatherhood, but also the responsibility and sacrifice. Selfishness, on the other hand, is that state of soul which, because of love of comfort, of self, or of possession, says no to God's will as to accepting and properly rearing children. Selfishness often causes a loosening of family morals, a yielding to worldly and sinful practices, and thus allows paganism to creep into the Christian home. Selfish husbands and wives prefer their own ease and entertainment, fine clothes, and the transient things of the world to children.

Therefore, the sublime and difficult task of child-rearing demands that you be willing to embrace self-sacrifice and self-discipline. You must have inexhaustible patience, deep faith and trust in God, devotion to duty, prayerfulness, and a right reverence for your children's human dignity. You must have a serenity that no reverses can disturb and that rests upon faithful devotion to doing God's holy will. You will not falter if your confidence in God does not falter. Such stability and unfaltering bravery is the ideal of every good mother and father. You must be so deeply rooted in the changeless God that your children need only your example and wisdom to become exemplary Catholics.

In order that you may fulfill your office worthily, endeavor to be what God intends you to be. You cannot impart character, virtue, and nobility if you do not have these qualities. You cannot teach respect for God, for religion, and for you if you are lacking in this respect. You cannot expect your children to be faithful to their duties toward you if you are unfaithful in your duties toward them.

∽

Acquire the qualities of a good parent

If you want to be a good father or mother, make every effort to acquire the following qualities:

• *Be deeply religious.* Religion is not only to be believed, but to be lived. Without God and religion, you cannot hope to meet and solve the problems and difficulties of married life. If your children see that you love God and your neighbor and practice your religion conscientiously, they will be drawn to imitate your example.

• *Be approachable.* You will attract and enjoy the most intimate confidence of your children by a sympathetic interest in their work and recreation, their plans and problems.

• *Be gentle, but firm,* in working for your children's welfare, regardless of their whims. *Firmness* does not mean severity. Strength and rule must be tempered with gentleness.

• *Be loving and generous.* Love your children sincerely, and be ready to make any sacrifice for them, especially in making home life pleasant.

As a Catholic parent, you enjoy, like priests, the greatest ministry in the world: the education of the conscience and the training of souls. Yours is the mission of fashioning the young hearts and minds of the children God has entrusted to you according to the divine Model, Christ. Try therefore, to realize the dignity of parenthood and its grave responsibility, and use the means offered by the Catholic Church to fulfill your duties faithfully.

∞

Chapter Twelve

Use your God-given authority to guide your children

By the very fact of your becoming a parent, God delegated His authority to you. You are obliged to use that authority to lead your children to eternal, as well as temporal, happiness.

When a child is conceived, God creates an individual, immortal soul specifically for that child. In cooperation with God, the parents provide only the material elements of a child. The child belongs more to God than to the parents, for He is the one most responsible for making the child a human being.

But God delegates the direct authority over the child to the parents.

He asks you, mother and father, to care for the child's physical development as He would care for it; to give the child the love that He would give to any product of His creation; to set before the child, as his reasoning powers awaken, His own divine purpose and plan for that child; to instruct, train, and discipline the growing child in all the obligations and means that He has made known as necessary for the attainment of his goals in life.

∞

Seek your child's eternal happiness

The primary goal of child-rearing is eternal happiness. The supreme destiny for which God creates, with the cooperation of parents, every human being born into the world is to know, love, and serve Him in this world to gain the happiness of Heaven. This is the very heart of the responsibility that He imposes on parents when He makes a child dependent on their authority, guidance, inspiration, and instruction for many years of his life.

Eternal happiness is the only absolutely necessary goal you should set for yourself: to rear and train your children so that they will want, work for, and win the happiness of Heaven. This is more important than to help your child to attain any degree of success or prosperity in this world.

Some of the important things that you, as a mother or father, should do are: to keep faith in God, and to teach your children to love and include Him in their daily lives; to teach your children truth, politeness, courage, initiative, and decency; to find time — no matter how busy you may be — to listen to your children, so that you may be sure to give the best possible response; and to care not only for their bodies, but especially for their minds and souls.

If you keep this first aim in mind — to rear and train your children so that they will want, work for, and win the happiness of Heaven — you will not be unreasonably saddened by any handicaps God may permit your children to suffer in regard to prospects in this world, such as sickness, early death, lack of talent, and mental retardation. The thought that your children were created primarily for Heaven will give you peace, for the things that look like misfortunes often make your children's attainment of that goal more certain.

You must, therefore, in union with God, want one thing above everything else for your children — the salvation of their souls — and you must work for that using every means in your power. Never fail to use the wonderful opportunities you have of practicing Christian ideals. Pray constantly that God may help you, and He will!

 споро

Help your children focus on eternal happiness
The first goal of child-rearing is eternal happiness. The second goal is a happy, successful future for the child. Naturally, you want healthy, happy, well-adjusted youngsters who will grow up to be fine adults. You have the obligation to provide, as far as possible, a clean house, warm clothes, nourishing food, and love and security for your family. But sometimes you may work so hard to fulfill your physical and material obligations to your children that you forget their precious souls.

Your children's bodies, which, even given the best of care must die eventually, may seem all-important to you. Your children's priceless souls, which will live forever, are sometimes pushed into the background. You would not dream of having your children miss regular immunizations to fortify their bodies against disease. Yet does it occur to you that you must also help the little ones fortify their souls against the disease of sin? Like Martha, you may be so occupied with the daily cares of this life that you forget that there is only one thing needful.[34]

[34] Cf. Luke 10:42.

Sometimes you may be inclined to train your children to behave well for purely materialistic reasons: if they are good, you reward them; if they are disobedient, you punish them. Wouldn't it be wiser to teach them that they should be good because it pleases their heavenly Father, or that they must avoid sin because it displeases Him?

If, in rearing your children, you have given foremost consideration to the first and necessary ends of life — namely, the eternal happiness of your children — you should also plan to prepare them for happy and successful lives in this world. But the true meaning of the words *happiness* and *success* is not understood in the same way by Christian parents and by many worldly-minded parents.

Try to convince your child that perfect happiness is to be found only in Heaven. Relative happiness, which can be attained on earth, is based on maintaining peace in one's life. Peace means harmony or order. If a person is to have right order in his life, he must maintain peace with God, with himself, and with his fellowmen.

If you want your children to be as happy as possible, try to build your happiness, as well as theirs, on a threefold foundation: the humble recognition of God's authority and submission to His will; justice and charity toward all their fellowmen; and control, through reason, free will, and God's grace, of all their appetites and desires.

Success in the Christian sense does not mean riches or popularity, fame or power. Teach your children to believe that the only true success is that which will enable them to render the most service to their fellowmen. Love of neighbor in action is the real object of success and the true source of lasting joys.

Thus, if you encourage your child to become a doctor or a lawyer or a nurse or a teacher, it will be because these professions offer wonderful opportunities to help others, and not only because these professions may make them rich. If your son takes a job in a factory, an office, or a trade, encourage him to become proficient in whatever he does so that he may advance himself; the better the work he can do, the greater are the personal satisfactions that come from it. The point of more money for better work can be emphasized, but this should be considered secondary in encouraging him to put more effort into doing a good job.

It would be sad, indeed, to find the hearts of your children empty and unhappy after they have attained material prosperity because they have lived a selfish, materialistic life with little time left for God and their neighbor.

The reason some parents fail to prepare their children for their adult lives and are not satisfied with what they have done is that they make subordinate goals primary in rearing their children; that is, they consider riches, success, or happiness in marriage the only ends worth living for. But the fact is that these goals are empty and worthless if they are not dependent on the true and lasting purposes for which we are created.

∽

Exercise your authority out of sincere love

Let your love for your children be a reflection of God's love. Since your authority as mother or father is a delegation of the authority of God, the same kind of love that God shows to all His children should inspire the exercise of your authority toward your children. All the commands of God are in some way expressions of His love, a love that inspired Him even to die for mankind. So, too, your children must be able to see this love even in your most difficult commands.

True love is a reflection of God, for God not only *has* love, but *is* perfect love Himself. Because the love of parents for their children is a reflection of God's love, parents should be very close to God. Reflect God's goodness to your little ones; let His holiness shine through you upon them.

The only perfect and complete test of love is sacrifice. Wherever God creates or awakens love on earth, He provides opportunities for it to manifest itself by sacrifice. Whenever those who love grow weary of sacrifice or renounce it, their love diminishes and ultimately dies. In a pleasure-loving age, the failure of many mothers and fathers and the delinquency of many children are due in large measure to lack of a spirit of sacrifice.

Too many selfish parents draw the line in making sacrifices for their children. They rebel against sacrificing time-consuming pleasures and amusements for the sake of their children, with the result that the children are left unconvinced of their love and deprived of many things that they need.

∽

Show interest in your children

Show your love for your children through companionship and deep interest in all that concerns them — in prayer, studies, work, and play. You are a teacher of your children with the special effectiveness that only love can add to the art and science of teaching. Your children are ready for its first simple ideas about God, Jesus, Mary, sin, virtue, Heaven, Hell, and prayer long before they can be accepted into any school. These ideas must come from you, and they are made beautiful by all the artistry of your love.

Assume your share of the education of your children. That means knowing what is going on at school, seeing to it that your children do their assignments, and helping them in their difficulties. It means being tolerant of new school practices. Children learn attitudes about school not only from their experiences there, but also from their parents. You can supplement the school program with rich educational experiences, by trips to museums, to the zoo, to your office, to stores, to games, to lectures, and to concerts.

As a father, you must be a companion to your children. It is through companionship that you gain the confidence of your children, prove that you love them, and open the way for their asking your advice when they are in need.

Give time to your children even though it is not easy after a hard day's work and tension. You will have a better chance of having your school- or college-age son or daughter for a companion if you begin with your newborn son or daughter. Playing with children is richly rewarding: building something together, reading to them, having them read to you, having a joint hobby — simply doing things together.

As a husband, do not neglect your duty to substitute for your wife in taking care of the children. Avoid the bad example of some fathers who will spend any amount of money to provide nurses and babysitters for their children when their wives want to get away for a while, but will never assume the obligation themselves, and the equally bad example of the fathers who will not spend anything to have anybody stay with the children at any time, but who expect their wives to be with them at all times. At least now and then, a mother should be permitted and encouraged to spend a free evening, or to have a vacation. Substituting for your wife will give you the opportunity of becoming a good companion, teacher, and adviser for your children and of fulfilling many of your other duties toward them.

Making sacrifices for your children is an indication of your respect for their human nature, and this respect presupposes love.

∞

Be patient with your children

Show your love by being patient with your children in the midst of the annoyances and discomforts that they cause. Remember that your children, born with an inheritance of Original Sin, have strong tendencies toward selfishness and actual sin. These tendencies cannot be brought under the control of reason, faith, free will, and grace in a day or a month or a year.

So do not be surprised or discouraged if your efforts sometimes meet resistance and if your children do not always measure up to the high ideals you have in mind for them. You cannot make good Catholics out of your children by force or severity, which result only in rebellion.

Never let your child feel that you hold a grudge against him or refuse to forgive his most flagrant faults. Even when you are bound to punish, the spirit of mercy should be evident in the manner of punishment; that is, when punishment has been inflicted, forgiveness is readily given.

The long process of overcoming the tendencies toward selfishness and sin that appear in your child will subject you to innumerable unpleasant tasks and discomforts. The excessive noise children make, their purposeless quarreling, their carelessness in regard to neatness and order, and their disobedience and lack of respect are tests of your patience and courage.

∞

Acquire fortitude

Strive to acquire the moral virtue of fortitude, which disposes you to do what is good in spite of any difficulty. It gives you courage to undertake difficult tasks in obedience to God or for the love of God, and gives you strength and calmness when God permits crosses to befall you.

Some parents are grossly lacking in fortitude. They neither exert themselves to care properly for their children, nor do they bear without complaining the difficulties connected with the proper rearing of children.

It is all but impossible for you to train your children in the fortitude they will need throughout life if you do not give the example of courage and patience. When your children see that you can suffer cheerfully and can make constant sacrifices for the love of God and their good, they will want to acquire the same strength. The child whose mother or father is cowardly, ill-tempered, or constantly complaining may gradually develop these same qualities. Day by day, try to instill in each child a little more thoughtfulness, patience, and self-discipline by your own good example.

It is natural for you to feel at times that the burden of sacrifice required of you is a heavy one so that you indulge in self-pity now and then. You know that to act like a child yourself, to give vent to impatience, to succumb to nagging, self-pity, and bad temper, will retard the development of self-control in your children. You can quickly overcome your feelings when you stop to realize that your sacrifices are your love in action and are accepted by God as rich sources of grace and blessing for your children. Your patience will be rewarded when, years from now, you will be able to look upon your children as well-formed Christians.

Love, therefore, is the one great means of instruction and training that God has placed in your hands. When your children see your love in all that you do for them — even when you must punish — you will succeed in carrying out what you have in mind for them. Lacking love, you will hardly be successful.

∞

Be a good example for your children

In all moral and spiritual matters, you should teach by your own good example. When good example is lacking, explanations, commands, and corrections are of little avail. Words move, but example draws.

By your instruction, inspiration, and good example you can make your children almost what you want them to be. You cannot, of course, force the free will of your children, once they have developed beyond the use of reason, to choose the road to Heaven. And yet, there is no power on earth more capable, by God's own design and with His help, of conditioning the free will of human beings for making the choice of what leads to Heaven than that of parents over their growing children.

You are a model for your children for good or for bad. They are dependent on you not only for physical things, but also for their first and most powerful ideas of what is the right and best way to live, of what kind of human beings they should be. These first ideas come not from teaching so much as from the conduct and example of parents.

If a boy finds home happy and learns to love as he is also loved, he feels secure and avoids misbehaving. If he can look up to his father as a model to copy, he will be, with few exceptions, a fine boy. And the same can be said about mothers and their daughters. All children are imitators. If you are careless or negligent in carrying out your religious duties, surely the little ones will not grow up to be devout Catholics. Delinquents come generally from homes with little understanding, affection, and stability, in which mother and father are usually unfit to be effective guides and desirable models for imitation. The way to have a good son is to be a good father. The way to have a good daughter is to be a good mother.

Knowing your power to shape your children's ideas of what they should become, you should make yourself an image that will always lead them toward good and away from evil. Faith in God, love of God, hope of Heaven, love of neighbor, patience in suffering, calmness in turmoil, self-sacrifice for others, honesty, moderation: these and many other ideals first influence the mind and character of your child as they are seen in you.

It is your moral obligation, therefore, to give your child a good example. Be conscious about living a holy life, and set a pattern of truly Christian living for your children to follow. Bringing children to Christ means that you must help them to grow into Christlike men and women who can take their place in life and stand on their own. This is to be done by admonition, but especially by good example during childhood and adolescence.

To give a bad example is often the same as to give scandal. Scandal is anything that causes a person spiritual harm and leads him to fall from the path of holiness and to end up spiritually hurt. It is possible to give scandal to your own children.

Jesus loved children. On one occasion, when mothers brought their children to Him, the Apostles, erroneously thinking He needed rest, told them to leave. But Jesus was indignant with the disciples and said, "Truly, I say to you, unless you turn and become like children, you will never enter the kingdom of Heaven. Whoever humbles himself like this child, he is the greatest in the kingdom of Heaven."[35]

Jesus is the champion of family life. His simple statements shattered completely the pagan attitude. He attributed to children a dignity that was unheard of until that time: "Whoever receives one such child in my name receives me."[36] He stressed the worth of children's immortal souls, for He identified Himself with them as members of His Mystical Body.

In defense of children, Jesus was never more stern than when talking about the bad example that can so easily be given to His little ones: "Whoever causes one of these little ones who believe in me to sin, it were better for him to have a

[35] Matt. 18:3-4.
[36] Matt. 18:5.

great millstone hung around his neck and to be drowned in the depths of the sea. Woe to the world because of scandals! For it must needs be that scandals come, but woe to the man through whom scandal does come! . . . See that you do not despise one of these little ones; for I tell you, their angels in Heaven always behold the face of my Father in Heaven."[37]

Our Lord hates scandal, especially scandal given to a child. Probably the foremost cause of juvenile delinquency is parental delinquency: the parental delinquency of bad example and broken homes; a widespread contempt for youth, ranging from birth control to gross indifference about youth's problems; and, above all, lack of religion.

We have youth delinquency because there are parents who are continually giving a bad example to their children at home. They yell at their children — sometimes for no good reason — but expect them to be quiet. They practice birth control, read questionable literature, and tell suggestive stories, but expect the children to be pure. They seek every comfort in life, look for an escape in television, drinking, cards, and idle gossip, but expect their children to be busy working around the house. They miss Mass on Sundays and drink too much, and wonder why their children can't obey when they are given a command or why they cannot control themselves on dates. They don't show respect for their spouses, but expect their children to respect them. They air their grievance for their spouses and for neighbors in front of the children and wonder why the children talk back to them and to their teachers.

[37] Cf. Matt. 18:6-10.

If you are careless in your duties toward God and the Church, especially by neglecting Confession and frequent Communion, if you fight and argue, if you revel in gossip, if you overindulge in drinking, if you use profanity, if you deliberately miss Mass on Sunday or do servile work on the Lord's Day, or if you tell dirty stories, you give scandal to your children. You harm them spiritually. The reason is clear: Children see you failing in these matters. They follow in your footsteps. They grow careless in their duties to God, to their neighbor, and to the Church. They will hardly be affected by your commands to do other than what you do. They may obey for a while when they are very young, but as they grow older, they will almost always follow your example and not your commands.

∞

Respect your child's personality

Treat your children according to the differences in their age, temperament, and sex. Every child has a distinct human personality, with his own disposition and temperament, with the special characteristics of his sex. Therefore, each child needs special treatment as he advances toward maturity.

Learn the individual temperaments of your children and direct them accordingly. A moody child needs encouragement and the building up of self-confidence; an extrovert needs discipline, order, and frequent correction; a child with a tendency to want to dominate others needs praise and, at the same time, humility; a lazy child needs frequent prompting.

But all this treatment must be given with love, patience, and understanding.

You will find both hard work and joy in studying the needs of your children as individuals and trying to meet those needs. Training children means bringing out strongly the good traits of their temperament by forming these traits into habits, while endeavoring to weaken the undesirable ones. A parent who knows his children and is willing to work persistently at their formation can make a good and relatively strong character out of any temperament.

Study your children. Behavior has a reason. Oddly, it is through the continuing study and increased understanding of children that you will better understand yourself and your neighbor. If you thought about your children as you think about your work — logically and objectively — you would understand them better.

Love your children, and accept them as they are. If you want your children to grow up self-confident, able to overcome difficulties and accept disappointment, and sociable and happy in nature, you must love them for themselves and accept them as they are.

If you constantly wish they had qualities they don't have, they will grow up feeling that they have been a disappointment to you, that they are failures. They will be unable to use fully those qualities and abilities they have been given. Whatever handicaps they begin with will be increased so that, in the end, they may indeed be failures.

It does not help to let your children sense your disappointment, or to compare them with other children. A remark such as "You'll never be as good as your sister" can be very hurtful. Much jealousy and ill-feeling in families, bad behavior, and poor work in school can be traced to the resentment and settled feelings of inferiority that develop in a child told repeatedly that he will never be as good as someone else.

It can be damaging to children to be social outcasts or to be last all the time. Your job is to help your children to become good at something, by understanding their strengths and their weaknesses. As a parent, you are the strength that provides for the weakness of your children until they are able to supply for themselves some of the physical things they need. Your strength should always give a sense of security to your growing children and firmly direct them in the way they should go.

∞

Exercise your authority according to your own role as a father or mother

Fathers and mothers must exercise their authority mutually, and each contribute what is most natural to his particular role.

You exercise your parental authority mutually when neither of you gives up authority or delegates to the other the making of all decisions when it comes to directing, correcting, or punishing your children.

Each parent has something to contribute to the proper development of a child. A father naturally leans toward justice and severity; a mother, toward mercy and leniency. The proper development of your child needs these shadings of authority.

As a father, let your sense of justice be tempered at times by your wife's leaning toward mercy. As a mother, let your feminine leniency be bolstered by your husband's instinct toward strictness. Let your children see that both of you are working together, complementing each other, in bringing them up. Let them see that decisions come from both parents, the one always supporting and upholding the other when the decision has been mutually made.

Settle your differences in judgment in private; do not parade them in the presence of your children. Never use opposite codes or standards of judging and acting; that is, one parent should not constantly shield and spoil while the other remains ever stern and unyielding. Then the methods of one make the methods of the other look foolish. The guidance of children is a task that father and mother should accomplish together.

As a father, you are to have a profound influence on the character of your children. A child admires and looks up to his father and is ready to accept almost anything from his example and teaching. Both you and your wife are the first and most important teachers of your children. You cannot resign or evade this function. Every other teacher is in some way subject to your teaching authority.

Never isolate yourself entirely from the business of training your children. It is easy to convince yourself that you are too tired when you come home from work to concern yourself with what your children are learning, or that you can afford to spend as little time at home and around them as possible. You cannot leave a job that nature intended for you and your wife in the hands of your wife alone. The fact that you must be away from your home and your children much of the time is no reason for you to abdicate all authority over them.

You should make some definite effort to teach your children, no matter how limited your time or how wearing your work. You can teach simple, fundamental lessons of morality; once in a while, go over a catechism lesson with your children, or show them something necessary to keep up a home, or teach them a game. Neither your wife nor the school can substitute for you in what you are designed to do.

Correction is only a part of your teaching function. It will be of no value unless you make positive efforts to make your children intelligent and good. Do not lay down such severe rules of conduct, and punish infractions so violently, that your children are stunted rather than helped in their growth.

You have no right to make all decisions and to administer all corrections and punishments without considering your wife's views; nor should you contradict her decisions without first consulting her. That would make her job impossible.

You should rather be ready either to administer a proper punishment or to decide an issue that perplexes your wife. In doubtful matters, your wife should be able to count on your showing an interest in the problem. The guidance of children requires much thought and much prayer, as well as the ability to talk over, simply and unemotionally, the problems, needs, methods, and accomplishments that enter the daily program.

Parenthood is difficult. Your work is never done. Yet, while you are creating as ideal a family situation as you can together, you will be giving your children a model upon which to build their own families. The glory of your parenthood will live on into the future.

∞

Train your children to respect your authority

Obedience to parental authority is associated with the moral virtue of justice, which disposes us to give every person what belongs to him.

Use your God-given authority to guide

One of the first and most difficult lessons you must teach your children is that of respect for the rights of others. The virtue of justice forbids stealing and all similar forms of injustice. You have an opportunity to impress the lesson of justice on your child as soon as he is old enough to associate with other children, especially by punishing at once the slightest theft and by insisting on restitution. Your hardest task will be that of overcoming your child's selfishness. Children must be taught that they cannot always have their own way — that wherever they turn in life, they will find themselves bound by obligations to others.

Virtues related to justice are: religion, which is the habit of rendering to God all the duties that man owes to God, such as prayer, obedience, respect, reverence, and worship; and filial piety, which is the habit of loving, honoring, and obeying parents and those who act in their stead. Other virtues are patriotism, gratitude, truthfulness, generosity, and friendliness.

You are unjust if you either practice or condone in your children any form of stealing, even in minor matters; if your life manifests no recognition of duties to God, such as going to church, praying, and respecting God's holy name; if you lie and even tell your children to lie for you; if you show disrespect and hatred for your country's civil rulers or break its laws frequently; if you are mean, selfish, unfriendly, and take your child's part when he is mean, selfish, and unkind to others; or if you permit in your children any form of resistance to your parental authority.

Help your children practice the virtue of filial piety. Insist on obedience and respect, especially when dealing with your teenagers.

Endeavor to instill in the hearts of your little children a deep respect for God's will as expressed in the Fourth Commandment: "Thou shalt honor thy father and thy mother." If you are to lead your children toward temporal and eternal happiness, you must teach them the true meaning of the authority that was delegated to you by God.

To honor father and mother means that children must obey their parents as long as they are at home and until they are adults. To disobey them is a sin. It can even be a mortal sin if the disobedience causes the parents serious grief.

Children, especially teenagers, must respect their parents as representatives of God. Respect means that you are not made fun of. You are not to be a topic of jokes, laughter, or biting scorn, nor are you to be called by your first name. Teenagers are not to fight and quarrel with you or raise their voices against decisions you make. They are not to criticize you if you are not as well educated as they and, therefore, make mistakes in etiquette, in grammar, or in the amenities of polite society.

You are taking the place of God insofar as your children are concerned. You act in His name in every legitimate command you give. Therefore, you have a perfect right as a father or mother to command your son or daughter, when out on a date, to return at a certain hour. You may command your children not to associate with certain other young people, not to read certain magazines, not to go to certain movies, and not to watch certain programs on television. In all these cases, there is no room for a refusal to follow orders — no matter what the children think. The orders must be obeyed. If they are not obeyed, a sin is committed. Of course, parents cannot command their children to commit a sin.

If you let your children have their own way throughout childhood, you will never get them to obey you in later years. Love for your children will not permit you to "spoil" them by catering to their whims; nor will love stunt them by unreasonable severity in its demands and punishments. It is almost hopeless to try to direct a child toward good and protect him from evil by beginning to exercise your authority only when he is advancing into his teens. As your child grows into a teenager, your authority should gradually express itself more often in suggestions, directives, and even wishes rather than in commands. This will work only if your children have always been trained to respect your authority and to recognize your love.

When they reach adulthood, your children still have an obligation to respect your parental authority while at home. Although they enjoy full exercise of the rights that belong to independent human beings, they must observe the rules of the household reasonably required for the maintenance of good order while living with their parents. They have the right to financial independence and to do whatever they please with their personal life within the limits of morality.

In matters of personal conduct not related to domestic order, those who have reached adulthood are fully within their rights if they follow a course of action differing from what their parents desire. Thus, if a mature girl wishes to enter the convent or undertake some work of Catholic zeal, she may do so, even if her parents do not favor it.

Teach your children who have jobs a sense of responsibility concerning money. A young man who has finished high school and taken a full-time job, and who may rightly begin to think about marriage and a home of his own, has a definite right to the major part of his earnings so that he may save up for the financial requirements of establishing a home of his own. His parents may request part of his earnings as long as he continues to live with them, but that should never be so much as to make it impossible for him to save any substantial amount for his own future obligations.

∞

Exercise your authority
despite other parents' bad standards

Your authority as a parent must be exercised in spite of the false, dangerous, and even bad standards of conduct that are approved of or tolerated by many parents.

Temperance: Bad standards of conduct are usually the result of a lack of the moral virtue of temperance on the part of parents and children. That virtue disposes us to control our desires and to use rightly the things that please our senses. The chief pleasures involved are those of sex and of eating and drinking. But temperance also regulates the pleasures of social life, amusement, and recreation.

Children suffer when their parents are intemperate in seeking social amusement and recreation. Persons who give themselves over to unchastity or drunkenness are incapable of raising children rightly.

You are intemperate if you are addicted to sins of impurity or accustomed to overindulge in intoxicants; if your interests are so largely outside your home that you have very little time to give to your children; if you take no thought about seeing to it that your children are rightly instructed in the things of sex at the proper time; if you permit your children to enter dangerous occasions of sins of the flesh or to keep company in ways that lead to violent temptations to sin; if you are not concerned about the danger that your teenage son or daughter can become an alcoholic if not instructed and guarded against the danger; or if you fail to offer motives and opportunities of self-denial to your children.

Sex education: Hardly anything in the upbringing of your children is more important than to inform and train them properly about sex, lest they follow the false principles learned from companions and bad reading.

As a parent, you have the primary responsibility for seeing that your children are properly informed about sex and prepared to meet the problems that arise in this matter. Prepare yourself for this task by good Catholic reading and study and by discussions with other responsible parents. It would be dangerous to trust that your children will learn all they need to know about sex from their teachers, from their companions, and from books and magazines.

Advanced sex lectures for mixed-grade children or public high school students are an abuse. You and other respectable parents should bring moral pressure to bear upon your school board and the school principal not to hold such lectures. You have a special obligation to try to offset the dangerous effects of such discussions in school by solid instruction of your own, with emphasis on the religious angles. Fanatics on sex education for children believe that the only thing necessary to keep children good is knowledge about sex; they are blind to the elementary truth that unless religious motives and virtue are added to knowledge, knowledge alone is more apt to lead to sexual aberrations than not.

When and how to discuss sex with growing children has always been a problem to conscientious parents. The following suggestions might be helpful:

  • *Do not evade questions or give answers that your child will later learn are false.* If you evade questions or give false answers, your child will be apt to feel that there is no hope of getting the truth from you and may seek it elsewhere, perhaps from doubtful sources. Always give a true answer, even though you need not go into the matter thoroughly when speaking to a young child. A youngster who questions you about the birth of babies is usually satisfied if you answer that babies are formed and developed in the body of the mother until they are strong enough to live apart from her; then they are born.

  • *Impress upon your child that he can depend on you to tell him all that he needs to know as the need arises,* and that it is only to you that his questions should be addressed. Tell your child that there are other things that you will tell him someday and that he should never listen to others who want to talk about them. Encourage him to be sure to ask you if there is a question that might cause worry. In this way, you will retain his confidence.

The attitudes of children and their later relationships with others of both sexes depend to some extent upon their early relationships with their parents. A daughter learns her first attitudes about men from her father. How a man gets along in a man's world is affected by how he got along with his father. A son will learn respect for womanhood from his attitude toward his mother.

Therefore, be approachable. Because you are a figure of authority, you have to take the initiative, particularly in matters of sex.

Stress the religious aspects of chastity and the seriousness of the opposite sins. Help your children to cultivate the will to be pure. Encourage them to use the means of grace offered by God for this purpose — namely, regular Confession, frequent Communion, and earnest prayer, especially in times of temptation. Emphasize the importance that sex may already be taking in your children's minds as a result of the frequent references to the subject in school and elsewhere. Try to provide or make possible plenty of the healthful activities and interests for your children that are naturally more appealing to them at their age than discussions of sex.

As a parent, you have the duty to safeguard the delicate innocence of your children in a world of naturalism and sexual obsession. Adolescents nowadays run into more sexual exhibitionism and sexual talk than is tolerable even for married people. Lewd literature does more harm to the morals of American youth than the schools are doing good for them. Movies, television, dancing, etc., present occasions of sin to the young.

In view of the ever-present incitements to sin, you cannot expect children, even in their teens, to make the proper distinction between the good and the bad, the dangerous and the harmless. In most cases, they will call upon the false principle: What is widely done is rightly done. The young are reticent; they do not easily give their confidence even to their parents.

Yet down deep in their hearts there is a desire to be guided, to be told by their parents what they should do and not do.

Pampering your children — especially teenagers — is certainly not recommended. But you must make some decisions for them, because sometimes they are unable to do so for themselves. Warn them particularly against the dangers of "parking," drinking alcohol, and reading questionable literature. Don't be afraid to make a reverent mention of God in your home. Feel free to ask your teenage son or daughter when they went to Confession last.

As a good parent, you must be concerned about the circumstances in which your children seek recreation outside of home. You are to know and pass judgment on where your children (including teenagers) go for recreation, with whom they go, and how long they will be away from home. Make definite rules regarding these points, and see that they are enforced from your children's earliest years to their late teens.

Girls ordinarily can set the pace in their relations with boys. Teach your daughter to be sensible and to see things this way: You can let a boy know you like him without being too familiar; boys who want to play "wolf" are neither funny nor flattering; keeping friendly and interesting is the best way to avoid an occasion of sin; goodbyes that linger are asking for trouble; you don't have to pet or kiss freely to be popular; real affection is too fine to play with, for it is based on respect, not on lust.

There is abundant evidence that freedom between the sexes is conducive neither to their physical and mental health nor to the success of marriage. Least of all is it conducive to temporal and eternal happiness.

Use your God-given authority to guide

Steady dating is prudent only when marriage is considered possible and desirable within a reasonable period of time, which may be estimated at about a year. Steady dating without the prospect of marriage within a reasonable time practically always leads to sins of impurity. Furthermore, children cannot acquire a worthwhile high school education if they are distracted from their studies by an immature love affair. Therefore, you should feel bound to forbid your children to date steadily at least until the latter part of high school.

You have an obligation to welcome the friends of your children into your home for informal or formal gatherings, because this is the only certain way to get to know the kind of company your children keep. You ought to chaperone and take part in such gatherings and enforce definite rules concerning modesty and propriety at all times.

God made us to be happy in this world and eternally happy in the next. Doing His will — as expressed in the commandments and by the voice of His Church — is the surest way to attain our destiny.

Do not make the mistake of letting yourself be swayed by customs, practices, and permissions that are allowed to children whose parents are careless in their duties or guided by wrong principles. Such permissions are usually voiced by the children in this fashion: "Other parents allow these things. Why shouldn't they be allowed to me?"

Try to make your children see that they live in a country that is predominantly pagan; that even many Catholics set poor examples of good Catholic lives for their children; and that, consequently, many things done by parents and children are dangerous and foolish. Explain that sincere Catholics have an obligation to be different from the majority. This kind of instruction can develop a healthy sense of responsibility so that your children will come to feel that they are helping others when they stand up against their bad example and dangerous liberties. Such instruction must begin very early in a child's life.

Parents are often to blame for the rebellious spirit of their children, because they give little of themselves — of their time, interest, and practical love — and then complain that their children do not obey. Let your good example be a sufficient motive for your children's obedience, even when you are obliged to ask them to do things that few other parents ask.

Because bad example and following false principles are so prevalent, get together with other parents who think as you do, and establish norms and rules that all will observe together. Such unity of action will make a deep impression upon your children, and they will not be able to use their usual argument.

∞

Respect the family as a holy union

Parental authority is impossible without parental interest in the family. The Catholic family is the union of father, mother, and children held together by the grace of Jesus Christ. Husband and wife are sealed by the sacrament of Matrimony. The seal of God has marked them for one another until death.

The family inculcates the great virtue of respect for authority without which organized society can scarcely exist. "Honor thy father and thy mother," as it should be carried out in the family, becomes in civic life "Support thy country and its constitution." "Get along with your brothers and sisters," as this command should be observed in the family, becomes in public, civic virtue.

Beware enemies of youth. There are three enemies of youth in modern family life: a materialistic view of the home, exaggerated individualism, and lack of parental interest.

The materialistic view is often acquired from material-minded parents. Ask an American youth about his home, and he is likely to give a detailed description of a house, with technical information on modern appliances, television set, and family car. To him, that house is home, fully equipped. Raised in our "progressive" society, the youth sees these things as the real values, which indicate a man's worth and position.

There is a great tendency in the world to judge others only by their influence and contacts in society and by their material possessions. Youth is ready to conform to the judgments of such people, which, in fact, are worth very little. Anyone whose opinion is worth anything at all judges others by their character and goodness, because that is the way that God judges them. If it were not for this, there would be little left in the world that is decent or noble.

Try to inculcate the following truths into the hearts of your children in order to counteract the world's materialistic atmosphere:

• The most important things in life are character, honest work, humility, loyalty, friendliness, and love.

• Never be ashamed of your home or family because it is humble.

• People who look down on those whose home is humble and who lack social prominence are not worthy of the friendship of decent families.

• Those who love and serve God and try to become saints will never be ashamed of poverty, will always have friends whom they will not hesitate to bring into their home, and will not be left uncared for by God.

Exaggerated individualism is shown by the tendency we all have to act and think independently of society when possible. It drives a youth to make his own rules and live and act according to his own code. Rarely does he consult his parents about his problems; important issues are hashed out among friends or taken to consultants provided by the state or community. The reason for this is that the child has never learned to love and respect his parents, because they have failed to show enough love and interest in him to win his confidence.

Lack of parental interest is apparent during the increasingly rare periods when the family is together. Personalities are overlooked. Adult members frequently talk over the heads of the children. Subjects discussed have little appeal for the youthful mind. Many children complain of being talked down to during family chats.

There would be less juvenile delinquency today if parents were more generous. A selfish mother who thinks she must work so that her family may live on a higher plane than their neighbors tells her child to come straight home from school and that she will be home later. No amount of money is important enough for a mother to let her child come home to an empty house.

If a youngster's mother is home, oftentimes he rushes off without giving any indication as to where he is going or when he will be back. Some mothers prefer to pass up the mental torment involved in demanding to know the child's whereabouts.

A father is too tired to be interested in the activity of his teenagers. He won't watch a basketball or baseball game or a play in which one of his children participates, because he has plans of his own: watching television, going to the club, or attending a meeting. When his teenager begins to date, he does not care whether it is steady dating or where his child goes on dates.

The structure of the home has been progressively weakened. No longer does it exert any real moral force. Today, many a home is essentially a combination restaurant and overnight cabin — merely a house. It has no stability, no contentment. It is characterized by indifference toward one another.

Avoid substitutes for the family. Who, or what, has taken the place of the family? Malls, movies, state- and city-supported recreation centers. Night clubs, bars, bridge groups, bowling leagues, and civic organizations monopolize parents' time. Boys and girls are on their own, and how they love it! Certain agencies have provided some supervision, but it is impossible for such interested individuals to serve as parents to hundreds of children unconsciously hungry for proper control.

Sodalities, drama clubs, and parish societies very often fail because of the lack of interest on the part of the young people who should make them up. These same boys and girls are interested in high school activities, projects of a purely private and personal nature, neighborhood parties and organizations, civic contests, and local promotional schemes. But they have no time for parish activities. Some become involved in high school fraternities and sororities which cultivate snobbery, uncharitableness, and an exclusiveness that can bring many evils, such as impurity, drunkenness, and carousing. Parents who do not encourage their teenagers to participate in the social and religious activities on the parish level are largely responsible for this undesirable situation.

Moral righteousness and effective living must come primarily from the family. We foolishly look for the salvation of our children and society in schools and organizations. A home is youth's primary need. Our salvation — individual and social — is in the Christian home and family. No man-made substitute can replace what God designed to be the cradle of character, culture, and civilization.

Try to make your children realize that the family is a strong basic unity; that, together, parents and children can find enjoyment and contentment; that they should look upon the family as the source of wisdom and a great guiding hand through life. Your children will see these features in your family only if you, father and mother, show a deep, personal interest in them twenty-four hours a day.

∞

Guide your children in choosing a vocation

As a parent, you have a major role to play in helping your children discover what God wishes them to do in life.

Use prudence. The responsibility of guiding a child to a successful future according to God's will calls for prudence, the moral virtue that disposes us to form right judgments about what we must do or not do in conformity with God's will and with our eternal destiny.

You are imprudent if you never speak to your children of God, of Heaven, and of the moral law they must obey; and if you never study important religious issues and the application of the Ten Commandments to daily conduct. You are imprudent if you entrust your children to educators who cannot or will not teach them how to act in accordance with the moral law; if your sole concern for your children is that they be healthy, possessed of material goods, socially prominent, and successful in marriage and business; if you fail to teach your children prudence by your example. By your character, your actions, and your words, you are largely responsible for the presence or absence of prudence in the character of your child. If you do not know how to act rightly yourself, or if you are not concerned about teaching your child what you know, or if you teach, by example or words, wrong ways of acting, then your child starts out in life under the grave handicap of a lack of fundamental prudence. You must, therefore, study to know what is right and wrong yourself and also to know how to impress your knowledge and habits of acting on your child.

Offer vocational guidance. After you have borne the sacrifices involved in accepting and bearing each child God sends you, He will ask you to give up each one to a calling of the child's own choosing. You should be prepared for this; you should not selfishly try to cling to the companionship of the child who has grown into a man or a woman. God's designs must take precedence over your own desires.

As a parent, you have the obligation to guide your children toward manhood and womanhood and to stand by as an experienced adviser when important decisions are to be made. It is not for you to decide absolutely and finally what your children shall do with their lives: whether they should marry or enter the religious life, or even whether they should adopt one career over another. Every human being must select his own vocation, with light and help from God, and in the final analysis, adopt a line of work in accord with his tendencies and capabilities.

In making such important decisions, your son and daughter should be able to look to you for good, sound advice. Sometimes such advice will prevent an inexperienced youth from making a serious mistake. You may never dictate a course that you prefer, nor forbid a choice of vocation or career that does not appeal to you.

There is hardly a more important counsel you can give your children than that which will help them to choose the right vocation in life. Vocational guidance is not a matter of a single chat between you and your child; it should be discussed from time to time in some detail. Do not leave this important matter to a chance solution. Do not consider it a duty of only priests and teachers to give vocational guidance.

Help your children to choose their vocation correctly by talking over with them the different kinds of vocation: marriage, priesthood or religious life, and single life. Tell your children about the beauty of married life in the eyes of God; about the sacred and serious union of a man and a woman in mind, soul, and body; about their duty to bring children into the world and to lead them to Heaven; about the unbreakable bond between husband and wife. Tell them about the wonderfully unselfish single men and women who live holy and useful lives. There are mothers and fathers, bishops and pastors, who thank God for such people, because they just could not do the work of the family or the parish or the diocese without them.

Explain to your children the beauty of the religious life. Just as Jesus once met young people in His day and said, "Come, follow me!"[38] so He says the same thing to your teenagers today, at home, at school, or at work. It is really the most wonderful life that your teenagers could choose for themselves. St. Bernard[39] said that it is a life in which you "live more purely, fall more rarely, rise more speedily, walk more cautiously, rest more securely, die more confidently, and are rewarded more abundantly." If you never show how much you admire such a life, your children will hardly admire it either. The mothers and fathers who are blessed with sons and daughters in religious life today are usually those who have prayed for such a blessing.

After you have made it clear to your teenagers what the three roads to happiness are, help them to discern what they would like to be, which life suits them best, and where they would do the most good.

As a parent, you are also obliged to help your children get into their life's work, and not just any kind of job. When one works at the kind of job he likes, he is full of energy toward it and feels pleasure in doing it. A day's work may leave him fatigued but with the feeling that he has done something worthwhile. Encourage your children to discover the type of

---

[38] Matt. 19:21.
[39] St. Bernard (1090-1153), Abbot of Clairvaux.

work that interests them. Even at age eight, a child may show more than ordinary interest in certain things. Special inborn abilities do not usually come out by themselves in time; they will grow only under encouraging conditions. If you find one or two areas of interest, help your child become better acquainted with them through stories, pictures, visits to related places, and speaking with people whose work involves those interests.

Never stand in the way of your children's fulfilling their destinies. God may call your son or daughter to the priestly or religious life. Marriage may be their obvious vocation. Never place selfish obstacles in the way of their doing what God wants them to do. God chose you to prepare the children whom He sent you for lives and callings of their own. They are God's children before they are yours, and you should willingly give them back to God when He asks for them.

If your children show an inclination toward a religious vocation, encourage and help them in every way you can. There is no better way they could live on earth; there is no life that could prepare them so well for eternity. Pray fervently that God may show your children His holy will and guide them in the state of life that will best help them to attain Heaven. The best vocation recruiters are Catholic fathers and mothers whose lives are an example and inspiration to their sons and daughters.

If God is calling your son or daughter to be one of His very special disciples in the priesthood or religious life and you interfere, you may be going directly against the will of God and tampering with the divine workings of a vocation. You may be preventing souls from going to Heaven.

If you are one of the fortunate parents whose son or daughter has been called to a religious vocation, be forever grateful to God. You should rejoice at the thought that your child will accomplish great good for God's honor in a life of service and dedication to Him and to mankind. You should feel honored if your child is called to follow directly in the footsteps of Jesus Christ. How many mothers and fathers are there in the world who would give anything for so great a blessing! Be assured that your son or daughter could hardly be in better hands than in the hands of our Lord. He promised that He will provide for the temporal and the eternal welfare of those who willingly make the sacrifice; He surely did not exclude the parents and their children who would share in the "hundredfold" He spoke about.[40]

Daniel Webster once said, "If we work upon marble it will perish. If we work upon brass time will efface it. If we rear temples they will crumble into dust. But if we work upon immortal minds, if we imbue them with high principles, with the just fear of God and love of their fellowmen, we engrave on those tablets something . . . which will brighten to all eternity."[41]

If you, as a conscientious Catholic parent, live by the principles suggested by the Catholic Church, and which I tried to summarize in these pages, you will join the thousands of good parents who are peopling the world with exemplary Christians, good citizens, and great leaders in society, in professions, in business, and in trades. But these principles must be the foundation of your own life first.

[40] Cf. Matt. 19:29.
[41] Speech in Faneuil Hall, 1852.

Chapter Thirteen

∞

Help develop your children's personalities

Each child is unique and develops differently. It is your duty as a parent to try to develop a balanced personality in your children. Personality grows out of the interaction of what we might call our constitution and our character.

∞

Help your children make the most of their constitution

Constitution includes physical traits, intelligence, and temperament. These three factors are important in developing the personality of your children.

Physical traits: In addition to differences based on sex, there is a whole series of individual variations in regard to size, strength, figure, skin, eyes, and resistance to heat, cold, hunger, fatigue, and disease. These affect personality because they influence both the way we look at ourselves and the way others look at us.

A person's reaction to these differences is very important. Some young people worry about themselves and are highly sensitive to what others think of them. Try to help your children accept what they are and what they cannot change.

Encourage them to develop what they have. Do not let them neglect their health by careless grooming, lack of exercise, overeating, etc. Do not let them dodge reality by being withdrawn, jealous, or envious of others, or by assuming a resentful, pessimistic attitude. Teach them to face the facts, to work with what they have, and others will accept them for what they are.

Temperament: People are born with basic dispositions that are molded through training and habit. Children can be flighty or stable, easily excited or calm, quick-tempered or easygoing, easily frightened or bold, affectionate or cold, demonstrative or shy. Try to stimulate prudently or curb various patterns of emotional response in your children. Be careful to maintain in your home an emotional climate of calm, warm affection, mutual respect and considerateness, and reasonable optimism, so that you may create a good environment for the balanced emotional development of your children.

Intelligence: Help develop in your children the ability to learn, to remember, to organize and plan, and to size up people and situations accurately. Your example — as manifested in your conversation, the literature you make available around the home, the qualities you admire, and the goals you prize — acts as a powerful inspiration to your children.

∞

Help your children cultivate virtue

The development of character is most important in the task of developing your children's personality. A child's character, including primarily a philosophy of life and acquired habits, grows out of experience and learning. A person has character if he is capable of self-direction; that is, he can choose his goals and standards of conduct and consistently conform his actions to them.

A philosophy of life: An adequate philosophy of life is the most important aspect of personality. Your child develops this philosophy as he grows toward maturity. It includes: a self-ideal (what he thinks of himself, what he wants to be, and what his purpose in life should be); a sense of responsibility (he feels he ought to work to achieve this by standards that are in accord with it); and an attitude that regards others as equals.

You cannot give your children a philosophy of life; yet, by gradually directing their thinking in terms of long-range goals rather than of immediate pleasures, and by showing them the need to relate their daily conduct to Christian principles, you can help them in this necessary development.

Acquired habits: It is important for you to help your children to direct the formation of their habits in terms of the goals and standards they have chosen. The strength of a habit depends not only on repetition of actions, but also on the attractiveness of the goal. This explains why some children who repeatedly follow a line of conduct while in school — such as the regular reception of the sacraments — do not acquire the habit of regular reception even after years of repetition. This goal — union with Christ, their best Friend, imitation of His virtues through the graces of Holy Communion, and the happiness found in union with God — was never made sufficiently attractive to motivate them. Thus they have not incorporated this habit into their philosophy of life.

Habits are important because they represent a kind of second nature; that is, once they are formed, we are disposed to act in a certain way every time a certain situation arises. Good habits are called virtues; bad habits, vices.

Pay particular attention to the formation of your children in the natural virtues, also called cardinal or moral virtues: prudence, justice, fortitude, and temperance. These virtues dispose us to maintain order and right direction in human conduct. Prudence disposes us to weigh carefully all the facts in a situation when forming our decision to act. Justice disposes us to give others what is rightfully due them. Fortitude disposes us to face courageously whatever obstacles and difficulties may arise in pursuing our ideals. Temperance disposes us to regulate in accord with right reason our natural urge toward sensual enjoyment, manifested by delight in food, drink, and sexual pleasure.

Since these virtues pertain to the chief areas of human conduct, take special interest in developing them in your children. You will teach more effectively by example than by word or command. Your children are careful observers of your conduct, and they notice any difference between what you say and what you do. Your work as a parent is to cooperate with nature and grace in helping each child develop Christian maturity.

Children require your guidance and example to realize in their lives the fullness of the image of God in their souls. This process is gradual and will make many and different demands upon you. In this sense, you must develop and grow with your children. In the process of raising your children and developing their personalities, you will receive as much as you give. And in all this, you need the grace of God to succeed!

Chapter Fourteen

∞

Help your children develop character

Religion should permeate the entire training process of children. It is a constructive and preventive power in forming their character.

∞

Teach your young children about God

It is a great advantage for a child to have his earliest recollections intermingled with religious truths. The sentiments of love for his parents are especially favored if they are associated with religious instruction in the family circle. Such qualities as the simplicity, faith, curiosity, and activity of his preschool years make his religious development a simple matter if he is brought into contact with the knowledge of God and His truths. You must provide this contact for your children.

Children are able to learn much about their religion during preschool years. By the age of three, the average child can have some realization of God as Creator and of Heaven as a place of reward for good children.

It is true that during the preschool years, a child's mental powers are not sufficiently developed for reason to play any considerable part in the training process. During this period, the principal method of training must depend upon the simple fact that the child will naturally tend to repeat acts that have pleasant consequences and to avoid those that have unpleasant ones, such as a scolding or punishment.

As a mother, you have the best chance to mold your child's character, train his mind, and influence his heart during the formative years. A child's personality is largely formed by the time he is six. You should keep a very close watch over those six years, standing in awe and humility before your God-given responsibility and privilege — awe, because six years is such a short time in which to inculcate into a child's eager, trusting heart a way of life that must be right and good for all of his life; and humility, lest you fail God in this blessed trust.

Ask yourself if you can in conscience turn any part of this training of your preschool child over to others. Art, musical activities, and dramatic plays are not of first importance for children. Regardless of current trends in child-training, your first duty always will be to teach your children to know God, to love Him, and to serve Him. This is not learned in a few set hours on certain days of the week, nor is it possible to instill it in a few hurried minutes of daily prayer. It is a way of life and must be acquired through ordinary everyday teachings and associations that direct the child's every word and action toward learning that this is God's world and he is God's child.

Try to make the best use of these golden opportunities for the religious training of your children during preschool years. You should try to bring the idea of God more and more into the lives of your children and gradually teach them their responsibilities toward Him.

This awareness of God, and our duty to worship and pray, can and should be started in the cradle. To hang a picture of the Christ Child over your baby's crib, to take his hand and make the Sign of the Cross with it, to have him kneel beneath a crucifix every morning to say, "I love You, God!" — all this helps to instill forever an abiding devotion for the Catholic Church and the Catholic way of life.

Love comes easily to a small child. His heart is sensitive to love and to being loved. Love, coupled with the wonderful imagination of early childhood, makes this the ideal time of life to teach him the things that really matter in life. Mother and child alike are made richer by this daily closeness to the Divine Presence.

Your own good example is most important. Your example will go a long way, because your child has a highly developed power of imitation and because he loves you. How a child acts as he moves out of the home into the world of school will tell how large was the heart and soul of the mother who trained him, how wise and prudent her love, how much time she spent with her child, and how willingly or grudgingly she gave this time. The everyday behavior of your child reflects your own innermost thoughts.

Children of six years of age can be influenced by the ideas of religious duty and religious motives. It is a mistake to carry blind obedience over into later years. Your children of school age are old enough to appreciate the reason for things, and you should teach them such reasons. Your aim in training your children should be to teach them ideals and principles. For instance, teach your children to obey, to tell the truth, and to be pure — not to avoid punishment, but because God expects them to obey, to tell the truth, and to be pure. Teach them to be obedient, truthful, and pure because disobedience, lying, and impurity are essentially wrong. If you teach your children the reasons for being good, their good habits will be permanent and sincere.

∞

Help your children develop good social skills

In the moral and social training of your children, you should look both to their happiness and to the common good of society.

Instincts: The foundations of character consist in the individual's inherited instincts and emotions. These are the mainsprings of human activity for good or for evil. Although these hereditary factors cannot be rooted out, they can be trained, their operations modified, and their evil effects forestalled. Although the tendency toward evil will always remain, evil possibilities can be converted into good. A person's surroundings also play a part in shaping his conduct, and surroundings can be modified or radically changed.

Learn what the fundamental instincts and drives in human nature are and what your attitude toward them should be as they show themselves in your growing child. The chief among man's inborn impulses are listed as capital sins in the catechism: pride, covetousness, lust, anger, gluttony, envy, and sloth.

Anger in children deserves special consideration. It is commonly caused by restraining their movements. Control of this passion must come from within the child. Self-control must be established very early in life.

Uncontrolled outbursts or temper tantrums are expressions of anger. They may develop many personality defects. Outbursts of temper may be imitations of parents who are irritable and given to outbursts of anger in the presence of children and who call forth severe reprimands. A child feels the injustice of such treatment and may even rebel against it. Never subject your child to unnecessary humiliation, teasing, and ridicule. Harmful social effects may flow from such actions.

When your children make use of tantrums, apply the following rules:

• If your children use temper tantrums to get their own way, do not give in to them.

• If they use tantrums to gain attention, do not pay attention to your children during the tantrum, but pay more attention to the good things they do.

• If the tantrums are due to some physical cause or to lack of play, remove the cause and try to give better opportunities for play.

• If you are responsible for your child's anger, control your temper, admit you were wrong, and correct your faulty habits. In the future, do not set an example of irritability for your children.

In all of man's inborn impulses or instincts, there lie possibilities for good and for evil. Their proper use is helpful; their abuse is harmful. It is important that they be controlled and kept within legitimate bounds. They must be kept under the mastery of the mind, the will, and the conscience. When these higher faculties are in control, evil inclinations will become harmless and good tendencies helpful. If you help your children to learn early to control their impulses, it will be your joy to see them develop into ideal masterpieces of the Creator. This, indeed, should be your foremost duty.

Emotions: Besides the seven capital sins, there are milder emotional influences of fear, self-submission, play, and love. Properly developed, these can help greatly to beget a pleasing personality; if not developed with due care, they may lead to harmful consequences.

Try to foster the milder instincts in your children. Encourage more amiable and humane emotions and desires that will counteract any hidden tendency to cruelty or hatred. Tenderness and sympathy, for instance, will restrain anger and pride.

Try also to occupy your children's attention. Play is the major interest of the normal child, and it supplies a vent for surplus energies and provides a harmless substitute for lower instinctive reactions.

The first emotions to show themselves in the child are fear, anger, and pleasure, or love. At about the third year, jealousy, cruelty, and self-assertion may be found to some extent.

Children should never be frightened unnecessarily. Those who are often frightened develop a sense of discouragement and failure, resulting in unwillingness to undertake anything difficult. Most fears are caused by some experience in early life. Fear should not become a curse but a means of protection. Legitimate uses of fear are fear of punishment, danger, and loss of the approval of God and man. It is dangerous to play upon the emotions of your children. Do not ridicule the fears of childhood; they are deserving of intelligent interest and sympathetic understanding.

Try to develop along salutary lines the pleasurable emotions of your children in the early days of infancy, for they are later to develop into love or affection. This will bring your children much contentment and will also make them a source of happiness to others.

Love of God and your fellowmen is the very heart and soul of Christianity, and you should cultivate it in your children with painstaking care. Love of self, or selfishness, on the other hand, is pagan. Diligently guard against selfishness in your children, for their earliest life tends to be dominated by their selfish strivings. To prevent the development of jealousy in your children, make efforts to prevent the growth of selfishness, especially by teaching them habits of unselfishness and the joy of making others happy.

A well-regulated natural love for your children is as important as the proper development of the emotion of love in your young children. It is the first essential in rearing children. Ill-regulated affection is harmful.

The home is the natural abode of love. With affection, a home becomes the most advantageous place for the proper development of a child's personality; without affection, *home* is an empty word. Love gives the home and family life its influence, for only love can furnish the motive for the constant, untiring care that parents must give their children. Only love can bring into play the spiritual forces necessary for the shaping of the child's character.

Love develops a union that binds you and your children together and fills their mind with trust, confidence, and respect.

This enables you — especially if you are the mother — to cultivate their feelings and emotions, the chief forces that determine character.

Early training: Since the home forms the first environment in which the character of your child is shaped, the family influence of the preschool child is of the greatest importance. Infancy is the best time for setting up proper habits of conduct. It is very important to develop properly your children's instincts when they show themselves even in early infancy. An individual's personality is largely formed during the first five years of life, especially during the first two or three years. This is the period in which deepest impressions are made, impressions that exert an influence upon the whole future of the child. At this age, the foundations of all later developments are laid. Use this formative period intelligently by redirecting and modifying, by turning their evil effects into good.

In the earliest years, bad tendencies are to be checked and social qualities diligently cultivated. Some social qualities not acquired in early childhood are rarely acquired in after life, and, if they are, it is only with great effort. The same can be said of unsocial tendencies that, if left unchecked, will soon grow into vices. For example, habits of ill temper may develop in a child several years before the use of reason.

Early lessons in patience and self-denial will do much to preserve a child from developing an evil and unsocial habit. Thus, it is not wise to permit a small child to do as he pleases with the assumption that he will grow out of it later. Such an attitude results in incorrigible children and unsocial adults. As years go by, the character becomes more pronounced and mature; yet it remains true to its earliest impressions.

Help your children develop character

• Teach your children to have a proper knowledge of their own greatness as individuals struggling for the salvation of their own souls.

• Teach them to love God during their young years so that they may more surely do so throughout life.

• Help your children to have a great desire, not for the necessities of life, but for the things proper to childhood. Do not stifle this desire by the addition of many material things to occupy their leisure, for this desire is one of the great driving forces of life.

• Let your children enjoy their childhood. Do not permit your grade-school children or adolescents to borrow from their maturity.

• Teach them to share in life's responsibilities.

• Help your children to strive for personal development and to know the happiness that comes from struggle to attainment through work. God will require of each of us an accounting of the talents He has given us. Perseverance is often the reason for success.

• Teach them never to gauge their importance by the material things they may accumulate along the way. Although it is difficult to stand against the current of materialistic thinking, remember you have grave responsibilities you must face. But the grace of God is sufficient for you!

Chapter Fifteen

⚮

Teach your children good manners

Good manners are the expression of controlled strength. A person who is kind to others and respectful of their feelings has learned the magnificent art of directing his strength and controlling merely animal tendencies.

Early in their life make your children aware of the enormous value — here and now, and just from the standpoint of temporal advantages — of practicing good manners. In good manners lies the true art of winning friends and influencing people. Lifelong good manners mean real popularity, with the later success in life that comes from popularity. Social and financial success is enormously facilitated for the person who knows the right thing to do and does it. Good manners are important, because they give us confidence, and confidence is necessary for success.

Point out to your children by example and out of their own growing experience how welcome the well-mannered person is in any circle. Let them know how much you enjoy visits by children who are well behaved, who have a decent regard for other people's rights, who ask permission before they touch things, who thank people after they have played with their things, and who willingly share with them their own things. Impress your children with the fact that good manners are not sissy, but, rather, that they indicate a strong character and kind personality if motives are truly Christlike and sincere.

Bad manners are not a sign of cleverness, but the clearest indication of selfishness. A bad-mannered person may betray a real stupidity that holds that the rest of the world is unworthy of his effort to win and retain anyone's friendship. Show your children how bad manners mark uncontrolled greed, selfishness, and even ignorance of the most fundamental human likes and dislikes, a sign of the most ungracious disregard for others prompted by utter egotism.

∞

Teach good manners at home

Good manners spring from the deep love cultivated by parents in their home. Only there can a child be equipped with the foundations of good manners — a respect for the rights of others. The display of good manners between parents themselves is the first real lesson given to children.

It is hard to don a new set of manners when you attend a dinner party or go on a date. Proper manners practiced over and over, day after day, become a part of you. They make you more thoughtful and more appreciative. They cost little — and mean much!

The home, often the place for letting off steam, criticism, and bad manners, should be the training school for learning to live properly and happily. But you, father and mother, are the teachers of good manners. Your children are great imitators and usually reflect the background of their parents.

Teach your children good manners

Children learn fundamental good manners from the way you speak to each other. If your speech is affectionate, if you address each other gently, no child can escape the influence of that example. There should be no jibes and no insults between you. When you want something done, ask for it politely. Let there be no loud commands, orders without "please," or favors accepted without "thank you." In speaking to each other, never use unpleasant or objectionable — much less insulting — names, even in jest, such as "the old lady," "my boss," "the wife," or "the old man."

Politeness is something spouses owe each other, and it profoundly affects the manners of their children. A civilized husband gives his wife the same polite consideration that any gentleman is expected to give to a refined woman. Your children should find in you the manners that marked your courtship and honeymoon. Their attitude toward their mother and ultimately toward all other women will be largely influenced by their father's blend of love and politeness.

These good manners are to be displayed in parallel ways by the mother. She treats her husband with the same politeness that she shows to other men. She is a lady measuring up to his stature as a gentleman. Through her example, the good manners of her children will inevitably be ensured.

Your children will be attracted by the charm of good manners as they see you walk these gracious ways. If your manners are bad and your training of your children's manners is slovenly or nonexistent, your children will almost certainly be rude and will betray "bad breeding." On the other hand, if your children have good manners, it is a public demonstration that they have come from a home full of love and respect, a home of charm and culture, where the parents were aware of the decencies of civilized living and passed on to their off-spring a knowledge of the proper things to do and the proper way to deal with people.

You can never afford to stop insisting on courtesy within your home. Good manners in the home are far more important than are good manners outside the home. Without the solid foundation laid there, on-parade manners are so much cheap varnish.

Kindness based on love and respect is the fairest adornment of your home. Keep love in your home, and God will be there, as the beloved apostle says, "God is love, and he who abides in love abides in God, and God abides in him."[42]

---

[42] 1 John 4:16.

Chapter Sixteen

∾

Raise your children in the Faith

Parents must use their God-given authority to lead their children to eternal, as well as temporal, happiness. You have at your disposal three means of directing your children to Heaven and to a useful and happy life in this world: a knowledge of God and of all that He has revealed; observance of the laws of His Church; and the use of the sacraments and prayer.

∾

Know your Faith and teach it to your children

There is only one means of attaining Heaven: Jesus Christ, the Son of God. If you are a good parent, you will want your child to be fashioned according to His example and to share in His merits. But Christ and His teaching and commandments have to be known before He can be accepted.

If you wish to preserve your faith, you must use your mind to understand the reasonable foundations and essential teaching of the Catholic Church. Faith is built on reason, and the more a person studies its bases, motives, and applications to life, the stronger will faith become. Some people lose their faith simply through inexcusable ignorance; they give it up because they are too slothful or busy with other things to learn how reasonable faith is.

All human beings are born with tendencies to evil as a result of Original Sin; these tendencies can be offset or weakened and replaced with habits of virtue only through the merits, the example, and the grace of Jesus Christ.

Now, no child by himself is going to learn about Christ, find access to His merits, and come to be influenced by His example and words. This happens only through his parents, and through the Church and religious education to which they introduce him. To make Christ mean anything to your children, you yourself must have been transformed by Him. You must be convinced, as St. Paul says, that there is another law besides the law of God fighting in the members of your children, from which they can be delivered only through the grace of Jesus Christ.[43]

Real parental love can be learned only from the example of Christ and practiced only by the grace of Christ. Without Christ, the other law within the parents, which fights against the law of God, is bound to be stronger than the unselfish parental love that children need.

As a husband and wife, you need religion. God had a great deal to say about marriage, and about what those who enter that state must do if they are ever to reach the unending happiness of Heaven. Christ transformed the natural contract of marriage into a sacrament that would bring special graces to those who would freely and rightly make use of it. He compared the love that should bind husbands and wives together

[43] Cf. Rom. 7:24-25.

to the love that binds Him to His Church, the love that made Him lay down His life for all His people. It is only through religion that you can come to know these necessary commands of God's will and find the strength to obey them at any cost.

As a parent, you need religion in rearing your children. Parents, by the very fact of their bringing children into the world, become actual representatives and spokesmen of God Himself. The very first right and responsibility of educating children rests on the parents and must be exercised in the home. Other religious instruction can do little for your children unless you lay the foundation in the home. Take notice of the following principles:

• The example of your life as a parent is the first exercise of your obligation of educating your children. If you are quarrelsome, profane, immoral in speech, and irreligious in word and deed, you are forming your children's characters in the same mold. On the other hand, if you are kind, self-sacrificing, religious, prayerful, and morally upright, you are laying the foundations of a solid education for your children.

• You must exercise your teaching authority by implanting in your children's minds the basic elements of religious truth as soon as they can grasp it even partially.

• You are responsible for teaching your children what is right and what is wrong and for giving them the proper religious motives for doing what is right and avoiding what is wrong. You are the first to teach your children that swearing, lying, stealing, disobedience, anger, and revenge are wrong — and that they are wrong because they offend God and must be punished by Him.

For your family to be an ideal family, all its members should think and believe together. From the earliest moment of your children's mental awareness, set yourself the goal of helping them believe in and think about truths such as the existence and omnipresence of God, the divinity of Jesus Christ, the authority of the one Church founded by Christ, the Real Presence of Christ on the altar of every Catholic Church, the necessity of prayer and the sacraments, and the reality of Heaven and Hell.

It is your privilege and responsibility to introduce your children to the knowledge of Jesus Christ; you cannot delegate this task to others. Make Christ known to your children at the earliest possible age. You can do this through habits of reverence formed even before your children are able to understand the reasons for them and, as reason begins to dawn, by implanting the first ideas and motives that make for faith and confidence in Christ and obedience to His will. This knowledge should deepen in your children as they mature.

Try to make Jesus, His Blessed Mother, and the angels and saints real to your family. Display religious statues and pictures in prominent places in your home, and tell your little ones whom they represent. Tell them stories about God and the saints as often as you tell them other stories.

Have a Bible in your home and read it. Subscribe to Catholic magazines and newspapers, and make them accessible for your children to read. Instill in your little ones an interest in good, worthwhile literature. Build up a home library that you can be proud of and that you and your children can use frequently.

Only religion can teach you what God wants for your children and how God's will for your family can be attained. Only religion can provide you with the spirit of sacrifice, the motivation to persevere in your efforts, and the gifts of understanding and true love that are necessary for parents, since they are representatives of God to accomplish His will.

Without religion to inform, inspire, and help you, you may make your children physically sturdy, socially prominent, successful in business, or famous in sports or the arts; but all the most important things will be neglected.

Provide religious instruction for your children

Your children need Christ, as exemplified in your obedience to His laws and your imitation of His virtues and especially His love; as taught by your life and by the teachers to whom you entrust your children; as present in the tabernacle of every Catholic Church, imparting His own divine strength and life through the Blessed Sacrament. You are bound in conscience to see that your children receive religious instruction.

Catholic education is important, because it teaches your children how to live in accord with the destiny that someday they hope to reach. Right living will assure the soul of everlasting happiness, and right living is taught in the Catholic school. Public school education may be fine, as far as it goes. It develops healthy bodies; it contributes to the stocking of the mind with all the human facts that are necessary for a humanly successful life. But it stops at the soul. Therein it fails. And therefore you, as a parent, should make every effort to see that your children receive their education from a Catholic school. The more information your child has, the richer will be his life. And if the information he possesses is of the highest order possible — namely, the revelation of God Himself as given to man when our Lord was upon the earth — his life will be enriched and blessed.

If it is impossible for you to send your children to a Catholic school, enroll them in a catechism class and ensure that they attend regularly. Most parishes conduct such classes for children who go to public schools. If even this is not available, organize your own catechism class for your children and others in the vicinity, and ask a priest to help you.

Your children can form a study group with other teenage companions. Study sessions could be combined with social activities and thus be made more attractive to adolescents. This would also provide an occasion for Catholics to mingle with other Catholics and prove a great help in enabling Catholics to marry their own.

When your boys and girls reach their teens, you must still guide and direct them. If you have given them a good basic Catholic background in their childhood, they will probably advance in virtue as they grow older. However, it cannot be taken for granted that this will be true in every case. Continue your children's religious instructions just as diligently when they reach adolescence as you did when they were small.

The moral and religious education of your children is not an easy task for you to assume, nor is it one that you can put aside until later. Each day presents a challenge that you must meet by the way you live, the facts and thoughts you transmit to your children, the values, beliefs, and example you give them. It is essential that you, as a Catholic parent, take a vital interest and part in the religious education of your children.

Reflect on the training you are giving your children. Is it sufficient to help them work out their eternal salvation?

∾

Observe God's laws

Try to make your children understand that to do God's will, they must keep His commandments. The indispensable rules of human life are the Ten Commandments and whatever laws the Catholic Church imposes upon them. Pope Pius XII wrote, "No greater fortune can come to individuals, families, and nations than to obey the Author of human salvation, execute His commands, accept His reign, in which we are made free and rich in good works; . . . a kingdom of truth and of love; a kingdom of holiness and grace; a kingdom of justice, love and peace."

Instruct your children in the meaning of the laws and why they must be observed. As soon as it can be done, begin to make your child see that our Lord's will and His favor or disfavor should be the measure of all conduct. The first sanctions that influence the conduct of a child are the favor or disfavor, the reward or punishment, meted out by his parents. Use this to instill in your child the Christian way of reacting to things, of dealing with others, and of coping with their own desires.

Offer motivation suited to the stage of your child's growth. Above all, set the example for your children in living according to these laws. Your plan should be that your whole family will live according to the principles that represent God's clear will and commands.

You must also try to develop in your child a horror for sin and all occasions of sin: bad habits, such as dishonesty, impurity, and disobedience; bad companions; and bad books. If you wish to preserve faith in your family, be faithful in obeying what your Faith commands. Sin is a direct insult to Almighty God, on whose good pleasure faith depends. God is all-merciful, but when He is offended again and again — so much so that a person's life is built on a habit of mortal sin — God frequently withdraws all His graces from that person, and the sad result is a loss of faith.

Keeping God's commandments includes practicing virtue. You should want your children to acquire as many Christian habits as possible even before reaching the age of reason. This makes the practice of virtue so much easier when its foundations are later understood.

A child is born with an inherent frankness, simplicity, and innocence. Preserving these virtues in your children is a full-time job, and not an easy one. But God will help you if you ask Him and if you really try to do your part.

∞

Receive the sacraments

Peace and happiness cannot exist in your home unless God lives there. Mortal sin puts God out of the home so that the Devil may preside. Satan's reign causes unrest and turmoil. The greatest means God has given you to prevent the reign of Satan in your home are the sacraments and prayer.

The Seven Sacraments are the necessary means established by Christ through which His redeeming, life-giving, sanctifying grace is imparted to individual souls. You must center your life on the sacraments if you want to save your soul.

Christ said that He would win for men by His life and death a new life far different from and far greater than the mortal, natural life. "I am come that they may have life, and have it abundantly."[44] This new life was to be a divine life, a sharing in the very life of God, for Jesus said, "Abide in me, and I in you. As the branch cannot bear fruit by itself, unless it abides in the vine, neither can you, unless you abide in me. I am the vine; you are the branches."[45] St. Peter calls Christians "partakers of the divine nature."[46]

Your life as a Christian, then, is a new life, a divine life, superimposed upon the natural life, invisible to human eyes. Just like bodily life, it must have a beginning, growth, nourishment, healing in illness, and strength for special tasks and emergencies. Christ devised special external or visible signs through which a person could know that his spiritual life was passing through all these phases. The origin, development, and functions of the life of grace were made visible by our Lord through His Seven Sacraments.

The sacraments are the source of your real life, the life that will make you and your family companions of God forever. Cherish the sacraments — especially Holy Communion — and build your family life on them; they will ensure the sustenance and growth of the divine life that began in your soul with Baptism. Let nothing in this world induce you to think

[44] John 10:10.
[45] John 15:4-5.
[46] 2 Pet. 1:4.

that you can get along without the sacraments; without them, your soul will die.

Have a healthy, not scrupulous, fear of receiving a sacrament unworthily. This means receiving it without sincere sorrow, or with no intention of giving up some serious sin.

Although the sacraments always bring grace to those who place no obstacle of sin in the way, the better you prepare for their reception, the more grace you will receive. Prepare well, by prayer and meditation, especially for Confession and Holy Communion.

Just as a man sometimes needs a physician to minister to ills of his body, and regular physical checkups to keep that body in good health, so he needs the sacrament of healing for his soul, which is called Penance or Confession and which serves as a regular checkup on the needs of his soul.

The sacrament of Penance not only cleanses your soul from sin, but also secures help (actual grace) in your struggle against the temptations of the world, the flesh, and the Devil. Confession frees you from and helps you to avoid the greatest evil in the world: sin. A Catholic should go to Confession at least once each month; otherwise, he will not be taking full advantage of the spiritual help of grace afforded by this sacrament. If each member of your family keeps his soul in order, there will be order, peace, and love in your home.

A sincerely religious parent and child will endeavor to go to Mass and Holy Communion daily, if at all possible. The Mass is the greatest gift the family can offer to God to adore Him as their Creator and supreme Lord, to thank Him for innumerable benefits, to ask pardon and to atone for the sins committed by each member of the family, and to ask help, spiritual and material, of which parents and children stand in need. Occasional visits to the church during the week are a great source of consolation and strength in bearing your daily crosses, as well as in obtaining rich blessings for soul and body.

Just as a man's body cannot live without food, so Christ says that the life of his soul will perish without spiritual nourishment, and He provides that nourishment in the sacrament of Holy Communion. Holy Communion — the sacrament received as a completion of the Holy Sacrifice of the Mass — is the greatest means you have of uniting yourself and your family most intimately with the only source of peace and happiness: God.

Holy Communion is a personal visit with Jesus, the author of all spiritual energy and of all holiness. He does not come empty-handed. He gives you an increase of sanctifying grace, which makes your soul holier, more beautiful, and more pleasing to God. He gives you sacramental, or actual, grace, which entitles you to special help in times of temptation and in discharging your duties as a husband or wife toward each other and your children, for Jesus has said, "Apart from me you can do nothing."[47]

Nothing can be more fruitful for the preservation of love and peace in your home than frequent Holy Communion. It will enable you to obtain a complete victory over the fault or passion that may be the cause of trouble in your home. It will impart spiritual joy, sweetness, and comfort to home life in proportion to the degree in which it is possessed by the individuals that make up the family.

[47] John 15:5.

Frequent Communion wipes away venial sins and remits a part, or all, of the temporal punishment due to your sins. It prepares a greater degree of eternal glory for you and your family. Finally, no prayer for your family can be more effective than that said after Holy Communion, when Jesus is present in your heart as God and Man, as your best Friend, ready to help you by means of the many graces He wishes to grant you and your family, for He has said, "If you abide in me, and if my words abide in you, ask whatever you will and it shall be done for you."[48]

Frequent Holy Communion (weekly, if not daily) is especially beneficial for teens. It is during their teens that children's passions begin to assert themselves, that the world becomes particularly attractive to them, and that the Devil does his best to establish evil habits of sin in them. Without God's special help, a growing boy and girl will hardly be victorious against all these powerful enemies. The attraction and temptation of mortal sins against self, of sins with another, of sins of dishonesty and destructiveness, and of sins of dangerous daydreaming and morbid investigating through talking about, reading, and looking at forbidden things are too strong in teenagers to be controlled and conquered except with the help of God. This help comes through actual graces given to the soul through frequent Communion so that the strength of Jesus may make the attacks of temptation against the weakness and inexperience of youth futile and ineffective.

Encourage your children to receive Holy Communion often, even if you think receiving the Holy Eucharist is a routine

---

[48] John 15:7.

matter. Our Lord Himself was conscious of the danger of the spirit of routine infesting those who would receive Communion often. He nevertheless gave us His Body and Blood under the form of bread — of daily bread — so that, despite the sense of routine, we might still receive Him often.

Pope Pius X,[49] in urging daily Communion for adults and children, answered the objection of routine by saying that Holy Communion is efficaciously and fruitfully received so long as one receives the sacrament in the state of sanctifying grace and with a good intention. He said that it is the desire of Christ, the will of the Church, the need of the faithful that all receive as often as they can, even though they are not always filled with fervent emotions.

Do not make venial sin a barrier to receiving Holy Communion for your children; the Church herself explicitly teaches that venial sin should not keep one from receiving this sacrament. Rather, Holy Communion indirectly takes away venial sin if we are sorry for it, and the actual grace received through Holy Communion will be a help to overcoming venial sin.

Do not teach your children that a small disobedience or a momentary quarrel will make them unworthy to receive. They will grow up to be afraid of frequent Communion. Of course, you cannot teach them to make light of venial sins. You may tell them how it must displease Jesus if children who receive Communion often do not overcome even slight temptations. You should insist that they make an act of contrition for small sins before they receive, but you should not go farther than our Lord Himself and insist that a venial sin makes a

---

[49] St. Pius X (1835-1914), Pope from 1903.

person unworthy to receive Communion without first going to Confession.

The best way to encourage your children to receive the sacrament often is to do so yourself. Try to receive Holy Communion daily, or at least on Sundays. Parents and children can give no greater proof of their love for each other, nor can they do anything better to ensure happiness and God's blessing on their family than to receive our Lord in Holy Communion often. If each member of your family is in the friendship of God and sanctified by the graces of Holy Communion, God really dwells in your family, and there is happiness in your home. Frequent Holy Communion, therefore, is the secret of happiness in your family because it brings God into your home; and where God is, there is Heaven.

∾

Pray as a family

Urge your family to pray together. Prayer is the first means of preserving your faith. All graces, in your adult life, come to you through prayer and the sacraments. If you give up the practice of frequent prayer, you will invariably find your faith weakening.

Introduce your children into the family's prayers at the earliest age possible. As often as possible, say morning and night prayers or the Rosary with your children. Train them to take part in prayers before and after meals. In time of danger or sorrow, resort to prayer as the first and most important source of help and consolation.

Kneel and pray where your youngsters can see you. They will soon want to join you. Start by teaching them simple, short prayers. The prayers you teach your children will mean a great deal more to them if you explain the meaning of each phrase and sentence, for they will understand the significance of the prayers and will grow to love them. Such prayers will make a lasting impression upon them, and they will think of them and use them in later life.

Urge your family to attend religious services together. Try to make your children realize as early as possible that in the Church Christ founded, their own family is part of a larger family called the parish. Go to Mass and Holy Communion regularly — daily, if possible. Take your children to church with you. Explain to them the meaning of the tabernacle, the crucifix, the statue of the Blessed Mother, and the confessional. Even very young children can be trained to behave in church if you explain to them that it is the house of God and that, when they visit Him, they must be very good. Having their own little picture prayer books and rosaries will help a great deal in keeping them interested and quiet.

If you come to church with a small child and he begins to cry loudly, take him at once to the vestibule. It is neither prudent nor charitable to let your child's loud crying disturb the congregation.

"Do we pray enough in our family?" This is a question that plagues many good parents, especially parents of big families. When their children are young, they are too busy and life is too complicated for much prayer; when the children are older, the best opportunities are already gone. God will make allowance for all real and sincere excuses when you do your best. He will supply the deficiencies, as any father does when his own child has done his best.

Provide in your home an atmosphere that will form habits of prayer in your children, that reminds them again and again to raise their thoughts to God, and that will lead them finally to "pray always"[50] in their hearts, no matter where they are. The following will help to create such an atmosphere: displaying religious art in good taste; providing a place for your children to pray together, such as in front of a crucifix; setting up an outdoor shrine; offering prayers in common, such as the Rosary; using seasonal and feast-day prayers; blessing your children, such as at bedtime or when parting ("May God bless you, my children, in the name of the Father, and of the Son, and of the Holy Spirit. Amen").

Most important is the good example of parents who pray much. What you do as a parent carries a sanction all its own. You cannot help influencing your children. What chance would a child have if, in the face of radio, television, movies, magazines, newspapers, and modern advertising all emphasizing a material way of life and a worldly culture, he did not have the example of his parents striving, however imperfectly, to live prayerfully?

If you are a busy mother and your family duties keep you on the go, do not feel bad that you cannot take part in many of the spiritual activities suggested on retreats and in sermons. For you, the will of God is clear. While your children are small, you have more than a full-time job, and carrying it out to the best of your ability can be a very acceptable kind of prayer.

However, a couple of cautions might be suggested. In nobody's life does God will that there be so much work that it

[50] Cf. Luke 18:1.

entirely excludes the opportunity for prayer. Even if you are the busiest housewife, you should cling to some essential practices of prayer, and count them as even more important than the household duties that are never caught up with. Morning and night prayers, prayers before and after meals, the frequent repetition of the good intention of doing all for the love of God in the midst of your active hours, and regular and frequent Communion are some of the indispensable duties of every good mother. Whatever you lose to work as a result of these necessary practices you will make up for by spiritual graces and help from God.

Never lose your desire to grow spiritually, and when opportunities present themselves, take advantage of them. As your children grow older, they can be trained to share many of your burdens. This will eventually give you time for some good reading, an occasional visit to the church, weekday Mass and Communion, evening devotions, retreats, and so on.

You perhaps never realized the tremendous influence the various doctrines and practices of the Church had in your own life as a child until you saw that influence at work in your own children. Catechism lessons, inspirational Sunday sermons, the sacraments, the Mass, devotions, good reading materials that store the mind with ideals and inspire readers to noble conduct, the great body of ideals that is the heritage of the Church — the ideals embodied in your patron saint, your guardian angel, the Blessed Mother of God, the Holy Family, the Man-God, Christ: these will influence your children in spite of all the efforts of the world. They will serve as a powerful and unfailing bulwark, even should all the protective social customs of the past fail them. Let your children heed the teaching of the Church; let them use faithfully her means of grace, and they will make the grade. Most important thing, let them have a good home and a responsible, virtuous father and mother!

∾

Pray for your children

There are few sorrows greater than that of good parents over a wayward son or daughter, even when they have fulfilled all their parental tasks. If this is your cross, remember that the natural feeling of disgrace in the eyes of your relatives and friends should not cause you sorrow. It would be a sign of worldliness and social ambition to go about acting crushed and humiliated just because the disgrace of a wayward child injured your human respect and pride.

You may feel bad, for social reasons, over the evil conduct of a son or daughter, but that feeling of humiliation should be borne as a special cross that can be more effective even than prayers in gaining the graces needed by the son or daughter for their amendment.

Try to find new methods of appealing to your son or daughter. Constant nagging and whining at a grown child usually accomplishes nothing except to harden him more and more against what is good. Try to be more perfect in every virtue yourself, so that your very life will be a constant lesson and inspiration. Your unselfish charity should move you to make suggestions, to give warnings, only when you have the confidence of your grown son or daughter and can foresee a probable good result. The important thing is to adjust all means to the aim of effecting conversion and reform.

Raise your children in the Faith

Remember that the first aim and purpose you should have is to get your child into Heaven. So long as there is life in your son or daughter, this aim can still be hoped for, worked out, and prayed for. No amount of sinfulness should stop you from praying every day of your life for this intention. There is an extraordinary power in your prayers, for such prayers have resulted in miraculous conversions and reforms. Prayer for the salvation of a soul is always heard by God. If He promised to answer prayers for even material things, how can He refuse to answer a prayer for the most important spiritual favor a person can ask for — namely, that a soul be saved from eternal death?

∞

Chapter Seventeen

Learn how to prevent misbehavior

What causes a child to misbehave? Most kinds of misbehavior are caused by one or more of three "bad" feelings: hurt, anger, and fear. Children's hurts are followed by anger and fear just as grown-ups' are. It is important for you to help your children learn to handle their bad feelings, and not to let them become hidden so that they pop out, maybe months or years later, in hurtful ways.

∞

Be aware of your children's needs

Every human being needs love. Loving a child does not mean pampering him. It does not mean buying him everything he wants.

If you really love your child, you must learn to know him as an individual. For this you must watch, listen, and find out what he really is like. Showing interest in your child's interests is one way of expressing love for him; understanding and accepting his feelings whether they are good or bad is another way.

Every human being needs to feel that he is capable. Do not expect a child to accomplish things beyond his years. Take individual differences into account. It is not fair to expect all children to have similar accomplishments. Quiet, patient observation of what a child is able to do of his own accord without pushing can be most profitable; you are in a better position, then, to know what he is ready to learn.

It is important not to overload a child of any age with requests. If you are to help your child gain a sense of achievement, you must be careful not to fill his time with what you wish him to do. He needs to have plenty of time to carry out his own interests in his own way. And his interests will differ with his age, his sex, and with the kind of individuality that makes him the person he is. Only he himself knows when the load seems too heavy. To be on the safe side and avoid disciplinary troubles, cut down on the "unnecessaries." This does not spoil him. It makes it easier for you to guide him as he grows.

Every human being needs understanding, which keeps down the ills. The worse your child's feelings are, the more he needs your help in handling them. If you condemn his feelings, he will not dare tell you about them. As a result, he will miss out on your help. He needs most to count on your understanding of his "bad" feelings. He needs most to share with you the things that are bothering him the most.

Love, achievement, and understanding are among the most important ingredients in a child's emotional diet. If you give these three in large enough doses to satisfy him, you will prevent many disciplinary ills.

You cannot tell, however, if your child gets enough of these ingredients. He can tell best. So it is safest to take his misbehavior as a kind of message that reads: "I'm hungry for more loving." "I need more chances to achieve." "I need you to understand me more deeply — the bad in me as well as the good."

⨯

Learn how to help your child help himself

Help your child to admit his bad feelings. One reason discipline so often fails is that parents do not take into account their children's bad feelings — hurt, anger, and fear. They deal with the bad actions alone. Dealing with your child's bad feelings does not mean that you ignore his bad actions. You must take feelings and actions both into the picture. But the bad feelings always come first.

Gaining a child's cooperation is a necessary step in discipline. This you do best as you show him that you accept his bad feelings, understand them, and love him still. Misbehavior is one way a child has of getting out his bad feelings. He has to learn better ways of getting them out; it is your job to teach him. If you are to do it effectively, you must help him to face and admit his feelings. If you can say his feelings out loud for him in an understanding way, he will feel safer in facing them.

For instance, if your boy disregarded your orders to clean the yard and mow the lawn before dinner and instead went out to play, you may insist that he remain at home after the evening meal and do the job he neglected to do earlier. His friends want him to go to a ball game. He has bad feelings of anger and resentment toward you. Instead of being angry yourself, speak to him in this way: "I know you feel bad because you can't go out to play with the other boys this evening. But you know that your father and I love you, and the only reason we forbid you to go out this evening is to teach you to obey us. You understand this, don't you?"

One of the biggest steps in helping your child get rid of bad feelings is to enable him to bring them out to you. As the bad feelings come out, the good feelings sprout. The "I know how you feel" technique is very helpful.

Anger at misbehavior never works because you are not helping your child to face and get out his anger. Your job is not so much to change the feelings, but to change the action, the misbehavior, that these feelings cause.

Give your child the kind of time he really needs: time for him to be the center of things, time when you and he are alone together and when there is a chance for intimate talk or for play. During this time, many things can be done to bring out the bad feelings in acceptable ways. When this time is set so that your child can count on it, he does not have to take so much time and attention during other parts of the day. No matter how young your child is, labeling the time as "your time alone" seems to carry special significance.

No doubt, you have made mistakes in the past. You have stored up bad feelings and let them out at moments in actions that were hurtful. If you start now by giving nourishment to feed the emotional hungers — love, achievement, and understanding — and directing the stored hurts, anger, and fear, you will have less trouble in the future. You will find that you can live in your family with a deepened mutual love and accord.

Chapter Eighteen

Learn how to deal with misbehavior

If parents would investigate their own attitude toward child-rearing and study their methods of fulfilling their obligations, many of them would find themselves fitting into one of three groups: those who are too strict; those who are too lenient; and those who are inconsistent or alternating in disciplining their children. Wholesome discipline lies in a consistent, middle-of-the-way course between the extremes of strictness and laxity.

∞
Do not let your discipline be too strict and severe
Discipline does not mean domination. Excessive punishment, ceaseless bickering, and endless restriction make the home anything but inviting to your children. The result is only too frequently a rebellious character or a silent antagonism instead of the development of a spirit of loyalty to parent and home. Deceit and double-dealing may be the means used to escape punishment.

The question is whether, under such rigid rule, children will develop a wholesome degree of moral independence and self-control. Once they leave their home, will they be able to stand on their own feet in the world?

Discipline is basic in character training and, therefore, also in child-rearing, but, again, discipline does not mean domination. Discipline develops control from within; domination imposes control from without. While there are certain "musts" every child has to observe, your children should be allowed to make some choices of their own, although not to the extent that they recognize no authority except that of their own desires. Some compulsion is necessary to fit your children for manhood or womanhood.

To develop discipline in your children does not mean ordering them around. This gives them no chance to exercise their own judgment. Punishment under such circumstances may bring obedience for a time, but its permanent effect is lost unless they really want to obey. When you do all the thinking, your children become dependent to such an extent that they have no chance to develop initiative.

Children cannot be ruled by an iron fist from the days of infancy. They naturally are bound to have wishes and desires of their own. Children who grow up in a home where the parents are continually shouting commands, nagging them, or talking about their faults in front of relatives and neighbors will often grow up with the idea that they are surrounded by those who do not like them. They seem to bump into opposition everywhere they turn.

A child has dignity given him by God. That dignity does not begin when the boy or girl has graduated from high school or college and brings home a paycheck. That dignity begins in the cradle and grows along with the body and the mind.

Learn how to deal with misbehavior

When Dad comes in from work, his wife would be unreasonable to expect him to take off his belt and give his children the beating they have been promised by her. Since she feels that the neighborhood children are improper associations for her children, her boys and girls have been confined indoors all day in a small living room and kitchen. Naturally, they are restless, and tension mounts until the promised beating happens. The father becomes the stern disciplinarian, and his children live in terror of him. Some children defy all authority because they receive such discipline.

A little child deserves more consideration, kindness, and patience. Some children get a hard spanking if they do not do what they are told to do, when they are told to do it. The parents' every word is an order. They are determined to bend their children's will to their own. Sometimes their wills do not bend, and they fight back. There is a clash of wills. The children's actions are often involuntary efforts to protect themselves. They flinch inside at the sound of the harsh tone, constant punishing, and complaining.

Such unfeeling treatment may have an effect on a child's whole life. Being crushed on the inside, children may later want to unload their depression on every person they meet. This could all very easily have begun in their early home life, when their parents kept them from fulfilling any wish or desire, even the most innocent and justified. They have been starved of human affection and later may reach out for it even though it may prove to be wrong and sinful.

The consequences of hard, unlimited discipline in early life are even worse when children begin to tell themselves that the treatment they receive is intentional and an evil thing.

They are so convinced of their own right to some reasonable freedom under reasonable authority that the constant abuse of authority by their parents warps their outlook. They begin to hate their mother or father and grow up suspicious of everyone. They hate authority and resent every order and regulation because they have had too much order and limitation as children. Other children accept their lack of freedom quietly, but they are always on the watch for ways and means of getting even. They become insincere, cover up their true selves, and grow in hypocrisy.

If you do not permit your children to enjoy their early years — with limitations and freedom reasonably balanced in their lives — if your children are reared by force and oppression, then they will be ever on the lookout for the opportunity of getting even. Later they can skip from one fault to another, their only concern being to keep their faults secret. Many other faults and sins — such as impurity, dishonesty, and cruelty — can be traced back to an overly restricted childhood.

Don't think your family is bad simply because there are occasional disputes and even open arguments. Human nature being what it is, those things are to be expected. But that, of course, does not make it right or desirable to allow arguments in the home.

When youngsters start the arguments and fights, step in and assert your authority with firmness, but tactfully and fairly. Cold, rough treatment generally produces a cold, rough reaction. But even hotheads usually cool down if they are approached with a calm, reasoned intervention. Harshness rarely accomplishes a thing, and persuasion generally effects more than force does. Remember, you have not converted a child simply because you have silenced him.

You may be tempted to force your children into molds of perfection that are not normal for this world, or to act out your unrealized ambitions through trying to live through your children. Let your children be themselves.

The ultimate purpose of discipline is to teach your children self-discipline. Discipline is to be used as a constructive force to help your children understand the necessity of authority. Start out with the conviction that your children want to be good but need help.

When you are a tyrant in disciplinary techniques, you may find that your child will become either aggressive and rebellious or timid, fearful, and overly dependent. On the other hand, coddled children get no bargain either, for the smugness and selfishness they have learned at home does them no good among other children. Therefore, you must be just and level-headed about discipline.

Nothing is more terrifying to a child or carries more the impact of anger and contempt of God than a parent's cursing, swearing, and using God's holy name in vain while administering discipline. What a harmful impression a child will have if he hears his parents call upon God only when they are enraged and curse something. Besides being gravely sinful, it removes the idea of God as a loving Father from the child's mind and replaces it with the idea of a wrathful, angry God who is to be literally feared, not loved. Children should be told that God will punish sin, but they must be made to realize that He will do it in justice, not anger. Be very careful always to speak of God reverently.

Why not begin to ask favors of your children instead of demanding them? Instead of finding fault with every task your children attempt, why don't you try a little praise? This change in your tactics may work wonders. Perhaps your children's attitude and actions toward you may change. Their actions will probably reflect yours. When you are polite to them, they are polite to you. When you are even-tempered and patient with them, they will be sweet-tempered with you. If you forget yourself and use a sarcastic tone of voice with them, say, "I'm sorry." You will notice that the clash of wills between you will subside and the arguments and temper flare-ups will gradually disappear. There will be a spirit of harmony between you. You will find that your children really are cooperative. All they ever needed or wanted was to be treated with courtesy and understanding.

∞

Do not let your discipline
be too weak or easygoing

It is not healthy to give children too much freedom in regard to their own wishes and desires. You cannot train your children by yielding to them and letting them do as they please. If you give in to all their childish whims as the easiest, if not the only, way of keeping peace in your family, you are little more than a servant to your children. You are simply leaving them unprepared for life. If your children are brought up to avoid what is difficult and to go through with only those projects that appeal to their sense of ease and comfort, they will be subject to many failures in life when they find themselves in a world of hard knocks.

Learn how to deal with misbehavior

If you give children too much freedom in regard to their own wishes, you will spoil them. It is equally harmful to give them no freedom at all. There is a strong parental instinct to let children enjoy their childhood to the full. This can backfire. For instance, if during the early years of their lives, children are given complete freedom to do whatever they think best about religion, and parents never insist on prayers, regular Confession, and Holy Communion, then, when they get older, any demand on their freedom doesn't make sense. They neglect the sacraments and even miss Mass.

Thus a child's first experience very often will determine what kind of person he will be for the rest of his life. If you allow the first experience to be that of complete freedom, of complete disorder, the elements of unlimited freedom and disorder are bound to enter the child's soul, as though this were the proper and natural way to live. These faults may well remain with the individual through life. This holds true for matters of religion as well as for ordinary conduct in dealing with others.

It is very important not to spoil your children. Do not indulge them with oversolicitous care. Do not allow them to impose on your sympathy. If a child becomes a slave to sympathy, he will never learn to face the realities of life. Do not spoil your children by babying them and giving in to their whims — for instance, to win and hold their affection or to keep them quiet.

Most children are inclined at one time or another to be fussy about food. But when you consistently allow your child to pass up a well-balanced meal and munch on candy or cookies, you pamper and spoil him. A spoiled child almost always grows into a man or woman who gives into any and all emotional demands.

The same can be said about a baby's crying. That is his only way of letting you know something is wrong. But when his crying is an evident display of the only passion he can give vent to as a baby, there is no easier way of spoiling him than by catering to him. Let him cry! Adults who display a complete lack of self-control may well be victims of parents who fostered in them that lack of self-control.

There is a tendency especially to pamper sick children. Although sick children are deserving of special consideration, do not make their illness so attractive that it offers many motives for not getting well. Even though greater leniency is shown children during illness, after convalescence they should again accustom themselves to play their normal role in the family and in groups.

If you do not insist on correcting what is wrong and insisting on what is right in the beginning, you will more than likely see in your children early signs of arrogance. They will talk back to teachers in school and defy all school authorities. This can be avoided if you realize what harm you do when you let your little child do whatever he pleases.

Children who are spoiled can likewise grow up to be brutal. In later life, they will be inclined to run ruthlessly over the rights and feelings of other people and be convinced that only they are right. When they were children, their parents taught them to be brutal by keeping them ignorant of other people's rights and needs.

Do not spoil your children by living by the false principle that pleasure and happiness are the same thing. You may say,

"Nothing is too good for my children." If you have in mind only material things — toys, playgrounds, candy, comic books, clothing — and if your idea is to make life soft, easy, and full of pleasure, you are making a serious mistake. The roots of happiness lie not in material things, but deep in the soul. Childhood is rich with all it does not own — rich in wonder, liberty, and freedom from the realities of life. Do not insist on filling the life of your children only with things that can be seen, felt, and possessed.

Routine play holds the interest of children for only a short time. But imagination, which opens wide fields of adventure for them, will keep them happy and interested. The constant addition of playthings makes "things" become the child's world so that he has scarcely a chance to learn his own world full of the unreal things of childhood. By the time he reaches school age, he has become used to material things.

The result of drowning adolescents in material superfluities is that they often become bored with life. Some parents have taken from adolescents the ideal of accomplishment and left them little to grow up to — and this creates serious problems. Many children are no longer expected to share in any of the work around the house. Yet it is this sharing that helps to build the finest family ties and to develop in them a sense of responsibility. In their anxiety to give their children pleasure, some fathers and mothers have forgotten that the family itself is the greatest of all character builders. There is no better school for learning the deep satisfaction of accomplishment than in the family working together. The fact is that youth has an intense dedication to an ideal and a readiness for sacrifice in an effort to attain it.

∞

Be consistent in your discipline

Inconsistent discipline is the most frequent fault of all and the most harmful. Parents who discipline inconsistently praise and then punish; one minute they coax into good behavior, and the next they scold; today they condemn a certain action, and tomorrow they pass it up unnoticed. Thus children hardly know what is expected of them. Since such parents are guided more by whims than by principle, the children may take advantage of their weakness so that they can extort bribery and affection when they want it. The result is that the children may even lose all respect for them and all confidence in them.

If differences in judgment between husband and wife are aired in the presence of children, they will notice the conflict and become confused. Such differences should be settled in private. There should not be two standards of judging and acting — one shielding and spoiling while the other remains stern and unyielding. In the eyes of the child, both parents will look foolish.

The type of discipline you employ in dealing with your children will have to depend to some extent upon the disposition of each child, but it must always be consistent, and in general must lie between the extremes of severity and laxity.

You should aim at a controlled freedom directed by understanding love. Try to encourage a proper degree of independence, initiative, and freedom in your home. This is necessary for development, virtue, and self-control. The opposite attitude of severity and repression hinders progress and may even incite to rebellion and the need for many rules and regulations, which are most unwelcome. On the other hand, do not permit your children to act entirely according to their own will.

Fortitude is important in the training of children. Teach your child the habit of facing the difficulties and realities of life courageously. Children who grow up without facing the facts of life will be improperly prepared for life's hardships. Try to develop habits and character traits that will enable your children to face the difficulties of life openly, frankly, and courageously, without self-deception.

Take the greatest pains to train your children properly. Exert your parental authority. Make your children learn from day to day that certain actions are possible or impossible, allowed or forbidden, justified or unjustified.

If you wish to rear your children properly, you must demand obedience from earliest childhood onward; but you must be sure to give more love, more interest, and more care than you demand. Your growing child must be reminded that, no matter how often you may have to demand hard things in obedience, your love, interest, and generosity far exceed the hardships of obedience. Otherwise the day may come when your child will feel free to hurt you by disobedience.

If you let your child do almost anything he pleases, you will someday have a spoiled and selfish son or daughter on your hands. Therefore avoid the mistake of either not demanding enough obedience from infancy on, or in demanding obedience while not giving your child enough proof of unselfish love and concern.

Try to win the confidence of your children without sacrificing obedience, and they will never break your heart. To do this, adjust your attitude toward your children to the changes in their age; make yourself their companion at any age, give them all your knowledge and experience as they are capable of receiving it.

You will thus prove that you love your children the way God intended you to love them. Try to develop the attitude of Christ toward children, and teenagers in particular. Learn to love them as He did.

∞

Learn the principles of discipline

There can be no training at a distance. You must go out of your way if necessary to keep close to your children and to enter as far as possible into their work and play. Today economic and social conditions tend to separate parent and child; whereas, formerly they were brought together and largely shared work and play. Now you must carefully plan and even sacrifice for this companionship.

The training of the child is not only the mother's task, but also the father's task. Since it is difficult for many fathers to spend much time with their children, they must make the most of their time with them. They must learn to take an active interest in the hobbies and sports of their children. If a child comes under the guidance of only one parent, he will be very liable to suffer a one-sided development.

- *Win the loyalty and confidence of your children.* If you are a trusted friend and confidential advisor to your children in their frank and open years, you have reason to hope that you will continue to remain so in the more secretive years of adolescence and young manhood and womanhood. Only if you are truly a companion, friend, and counselor of your children will they bring all their problems, troubles, and doubts to you for solutions.

• *Give your children as few commands as possible.* They resent domination and overcorrection as much as you do.

Before you give a command to your child, be sure to secure his attention. Attention is necessary for real cooperation. Children who are at play and absorbed in what they are doing will hardly recognize or heed an order shouted to them on the spur of the moment.

Follow up the commands you give your children. Let them know firmly but kindly that you unfailingly expect obedience. Discipline is undermined by a spirit of disobedience.

• *Do not expect the impossible of your children.* If your commands are reasonable, your children will find obedience fairly easy.

• *Never make use of threats to force your children to obey.* This results in filling the hearts of your children with fear. It may convince them that your commands are not too important.

• *Never deceive your children.* If they discover the deception, their confidence in you will suffer, and it will not be easily restored.

• *Be just in dealing with your children.* Injustice, if recognized, will lessen your children's respect for you and their confidence in you.

• *Approve the good acts of your children, as you condemn the bad ones.* Thus, if you reprove your children for eating too much candy, commend them when they eat vegetables and fruits. It is very important to give a positive rather than a negative turn to your efforts in training your children.

Chapter Nineteen

ༀ

Use punishment prudently

At times a mild form of punishment may become necessary in training your children within the home. Its aim should always be to bring about regret in their mind; that is, they should feel sorry for their misdemeanor. The result should be that they will not readily repeat it. No punishment is more disputed than physical punishment, or spanking, and none is more abused.

Before your children reach the age of reason, spanking may be necessary. Small children cannot be expected to understand the consequences of wrong behavior as an adult would. They can, however, understand pain. They may not realize the danger of playing in the street, but if they are swatted, they are able to associate the pain with the danger. It is better to spank them than risk their getting hit by a car.

In the case of the average child, use of corporal punishment is not commendable. It is hard to punish unemotionally and harder still to receive punishment in that manner. Corporal punishment may more easily make your children defiant or secretive rather than penitent.

Spanking rarely, if ever, should be used after your child has reached the age of reason. This does not mean that punishment is no longer necessary. But it should conform to the child's new sense of individual dignity. Spanking may cause a strong-willed child to become even more set in his ways. But reasonable punishment, such as taking away certain privileges, enables him to see his error without doing harm to his dignity as a person.

Bodily punishment seems to ignore this spiritual dignity because it implies that behavior must be controlled by appealing to animal instincts and to the physical senses. Since your child has a mind that thinks, a will that is free, and a soul that is immortal, he should be treated like a human being. Give him the same respect and consideration that elders demand.

If you must punish your children, let the punishment be constructive; that is, let it be rational, not emotional; temperate, not vengeful. Don't try to get even with your children for some irritation caused by their behavior. Never impose any kind of punishment for the purpose of breaking their will, but rather out of a real concern.

Punishment should follow naturally from the offense committed. This will make your children see the consequence of their own act rather than your anger or resentment.

◿

Learn to punish constructively
• *Do not punish your children in anger.* If you are angry, you cannot trust yourself to correct another person, because your anger is likely to cause you to be too severe. You cannot exercise good judgment. Angry punishment leaves your children feeling that your wishes have been forced upon them. Try to show your children,

even in the midst of correcting them and punishing them, that you are solely interested in their welfare, and that you are motivated far more by love than by anger.

• *Do not humiliate your children.* Such treatment undermines their feeling of importance as persons and weakens their sense of security. They must depend upon you for love and cannot be left on their own. To belittle them is one way of making them lose confidence in you, for they cannot trust your love for them. Therefore, don't speak to others of your children's faults or bad conduct as amusing or humorous in their presence.

• *Do not punish by refusing to keep a promise.* Your promises should always be kept. If you have told your child that he may go to a picnic tomorrow, do not punish him by refusing to let him go. You will hardly influence his behavior unless you are able to win and hold his confidence. Breaking your promise tends to weaken his confidence in you.

• *Do not punish for personal satisfaction.* If you punish your children to relieve your own pent-up feelings or to assert your authority, you do not really have their interest at heart.

As your children grow from babyhood to boyhood or girlhood, they become more and more aware that they are persons with dignity. They discover their new willfulness and they want to assert themselves. If you make a threatening demand, they may hesitate before acting even though they understand its reasonableness. They may even complain. You may think they are stubborn, but this may be their way of asserting their own importance.

Obedience is necessary and must be insisted upon, but there is such a thing as being too strict. Considerable patience is required in training boys and girls at this period of their development. It is better not to make too many demands. Their contrariness is a phase of their personality growth. It will pass in time without harmful effects if you are patient and understanding.

• *Do not punish with harsh words.* Threats and verbal abuse may make your children do your will, but they leave upon their minds marks that are like scars. Physical pain passes and is forgotten, but it is difficult to forget the mental pain caused by a vicious tongue. And when the threat is repeated, but not carried out, it becomes meaningless; your children know that nothing will happen. Idle threats may encourage them to see how far they can go without obeying your orders.

The practice of using threats is bad even when failure to obey is followed by punishment. Children who act under a threat are driven just as surely as if they were whipped. Their obedience is due to helplessness, not to any real desire to cooperate. Inwardly they rebel.

Harsh remarks are also ineffective and even harmful. Such words do not encourage enthusiasm, but destroy self-confidence. They may even give the children a feeling of inferiority.

• *Do not punish too severely or too frequently.* Discretion should be the rule. When the punishment is overdone, its force is lost and it becomes a price to be paid for your children to do what they want. If they feel the price is not too high, they will really accept the risk.

Make a distinction in the severity of your corrections, according to the degree of misbehavior. Do not use physical punishment too frequently or violently, thus making your children's fear of you far greater than their love. Your children need encouragement if they are to grow as normal children should. Indiscriminate and frequent punishment focuses attention on their mistakes and gives them a sense of failure.

• *Punish with sufficient explanation.* Administering physical punishment can be harmful if this method of correction is used either too often or with anger, ill-temper, or cruelty.

Excluding such extremes, there is a place for bodily punishment in the rearing of a child. Reserve such a method for more serious faults or persistent small faults that nothing else has seemed sufficient to cure. Accompany it by sufficient explanation to make your child realize that its purpose is to make memorable the lesson that you want to teach, and that it should hurt without harming. Make your child understand that it is a very unpleasant thing for you and that your having to punish in no way lessens your love for him.

• *Do not punish your children by depriving them of anything necessary for their well-being.* For instance, do not send them to bed without their evening meal; they need their food and sleep.

• *Do not punish your children by giving them work to do,* because work is not to be considered a punishment but a noble action. The lesson of work is one we all must learn; we can't avoid it by being good. Using work as a punishment may deprive your child of an honest liking for it.

Suppose your little son is playing carelessly with a ball. You tell him to stop before he breaks a window. He doesn't pay any attention to you, and he breaks the window. You can explain to your son the seriousness of his disobedience because a new pane of glass will cost money and people have to work for money. You may have paid your boy for doing extra work around the home. You now explain to him that he must do extra work without pay until he has earned enough to replace the broken glass. In this way, he is not only impressed with the necessity of obedience; he is also brought to understand the necessity of work.

By assigning a task in this way, you are putting the punishment on a high level. You are using work as a means of instilling a sense of personal responsibility, something far different from insisting on work as a punishment for the misdemeanor. This is constructive, because it teaches your boy the necessity of both obedience and work.

• *Do not postpone punishment.* To do this leaves your children to suffer all sorts of imagined worries and fears.

Punishment should teach a lesson. For this reason, punishment and the reason for it should be as closely linked as possible. If you postpone punishment, the misdeed will have become so remote that the value of punishment will be lost.

• *Do not fail to punish your children because of inordinate love or soft-heartedness or laziness, when punishment is the only means to teach them an important lesson.* Don't show favoritism toward one of your children, especially in the matter of correction and punishment. Don't defend your children against people who complain about their actual faults or misconduct.

Effective child-training avoids extremes. It should take a middle course in which compulsion and love are blended. It begins with a child's interests and ends in the child's development as a responsible man or woman.

Chapter Twenty

∽

Discipline your teenagers wisely

Teenagers are naturally inexperienced in many areas of life. They have not yet faced the difficulties to be met in carrying out life's plans. They have not yet been hurt by the failures that teach a certain amount of caution. Young people must find out for themselves by doing, or at least by trying.

Contrasts between the members of two generations are evident. Whereas youth is daring, parents tend to be cautious, because they have lived long enough to know the dangers that lurk behind many attractive undertakings. They have been hurt often enough to keep away from painful experiences. They tend not only to be cautious themselves but also to caution youth to be careful.

Whereas youth is explorative, parents tend to be conservative. By the time a person is old enough to have children, he is ready to settle down and to protect his holdings. He enjoys a quiet evening at home. He has responsibilities that must be met, children who must be cared for, property to be protected, and interests to be safeguarded.

Whereas young people are primarily interested in others their own age, parents remain interested in their children.

The widespread effort of parents to keep young tends to make them try to hold on to their children at the very time when youth is striving to be independent.

Today the young man or woman faces literally thousands of vocational possibilities. Recreational opportunities have similarly increased. The choices are many and confusing. Out of the variety of opportunities open to youth comes the problem of making wise choices, not only of where to go and what to do, but even of what to be. Everyday conflicts with teenagers are common in the modern family. The question is how to reduce conflict.

∞

Set curfews

You and your teenagers should agree that the hour for their getting in on school nights should be earlier and more strictly observed than may be necessary for weekend evenings out.

Sensible parents doubt the advisability of allowing young people out at all on school nights. Since a school day is long and strenuous, evenings are the only time available for doing homework, engaging in hobbies, being with family, and getting the relaxation that teenagers need. But high school students are often involved in community centers, clubs, plays, school sports, and church functions. Granted that your concern about sleep and homework cannot be ignored and that your teenagers have social obligations and opportunities that must sometimes take them out on school nights, parents and teenagers should agree on when teenagers must return home.

If your teenagers go out on Friday and Saturday evenings, when the problems of homework and sleep are not so pressing, they should let you know where the event is, who is going, what is going to happen, when it is expected to be over, how the trip home is to be made, and whether you will be notified if the hour is to be later than expected or if your help is needed. When you and your teenagers have mutual confidence in each other, such questions as these can be discussed beforehand and with the result that you are reassured enough to put you and your children at ease. Young people who can share with their parents enough of what happens when they are out, what makes them late from time to time, and how they themselves feel about it, help their parents gain a real understanding of the world of youth, which they need and want.

If you are not too rigid, you are often able to build up in your teenagers a sense of responsibility and the ability to take care of themselves wherever they are. Mutual trust, which is so essential, can too often be marred by bickering over the time for getting in at night. And yet, be deeply conscious of your responsibility to know where, how, and with whom your children spend their leisure hours.

§

Teach your teenagers how to spend money wisely
Train your children to do things in and for the family and the home out of love, and not on the basis of a kind of wage-contract. If you have brought up your children to expect payment for washing dishes or for babysitting, you will find it difficult to teach them to do it cheerfully for love.

Let your children sometimes enjoy being rewarded for what they do. But instead of giving them a specific amount for a specific task done, offer them unexpected gifts at various times. It is a good idea to have family outings or treats in recognition of work done for your family by your children. Thus the work that is done as a part of your family is rewarded through your whole family's enjoyment. Do not count the value of everything in terms of money, and do not teach your children to do so.

Most young people today have more money to spend than their parents had at their age, and they have more to spend it on, too. The problem will not be met by criticizing young people for having more money or by restricting their use of it, but rather by helping them to assume responsibility for what they have. The allowance system, under which parents give a stipulated sum to each of their children regularly to take care of personal expenses, is becoming a general practice. The allowance can be determined by considering these factors: For what does your child need money (dues, lunches, transportation)? What is the allowance expected to cover (clothing, movies, books)? How much previous experience has your child had with money? What will the family budget allow easily?

Once an allowance is agreed upon, it is up to your child to be responsible for it. If he cannot make it cover his expenses without frequent loans and supplements, review the whole situation.

Give your children as much freedom as they can take responsibility for. If one youngster has learned how to earn, spend, and save money, you may allow him more freedom than one who has had little experience in earning and spending. You need not be too severe in restricting your child's spending of his earnings unless he shows signs of being in trouble or in need of more direct supervision.

∞

Teach your teenagers to take care of things

Teenagers should be taught to assume responsibility for the care of personal and family property. But responsibility must be given before it is taken. As a parent, you must take responsibility for your own life in ways that are satisfying, and you must leave your children free to assume increasing responsibility for theirs. This will provide a wholesome atmosphere for growth in responsibility through the years.

The son or daughter whose room is his to do with as he will has a better chance of learning to take care of it. If he is free to choose how his room will be furnished, if he is free to bring his friends there without question, if he can leave his projects undisturbed when he goes out, he will feel that it is his own and keep it in a way that satisfies him and that meets the standards that he has learned at home. But the smothering mother who hovers nearby to remind her teenager to find his school books, to hang up his clothes, or to scrub the tub often ends up doing the job herself. This undermines training in personal responsibility.

Let your teenage children run their own affairs; they will take as much responsibility as is really theirs. Young people who plan and build their own recreation centers and have the responsibility of running them thereafter have no difficulty in protecting the property. Young people who are made to feel at home in school, with student controls and activities planned by and for students, take pride in their school and protect it with enthusiastic care. Priests have found that young people assume more reverence when more appreciative respect is shown them through participation in youth choirs, study clubs, youth religious devotions, and other programs geared to meet their needs and interests.

Adult hostility toward youth kindles feelings of resentment. Youth's destructiveness often stems from feeling neglected, ignored, left out, and perpetually criticized. As more and more communities have accepted the younger generation with appreciation and respect, young people have responded with enthusiastic cooperation.

∽

Encourage your teenagers
to help with household work

Teach your children from earliest childhood to take some active part in the work of keeping up a home and running a family. Although their contribution is small, look on it as important. In their own home, and under the motivation of family love, your children can best learn to share responsibility, to make sacrifices, and to love to do things for others. This training will have a deep influence on their adult lives.

Teenagers are expected to do their school work and their share of the work that must be done around the house. If you are a conscientious parent, you will see that your teenagers do several types of work, not only because it must be done, but also because youth must be taught responsibility for such things.

Your teenagers will take their share of the day-to-day jobs around your house if they feel that they have a real stake in the family; if they know that their efforts will be noticed and appreciated; if they recognize that the others of the family are pulling their share of the load; and if they are free to do the jobs themselves in their own way and without too much supervision.

This does not mean that you should not guide youngsters, but there are good ways of doing this and ways that should be avoided. If you keep a string on all the household responsibilities, laying down minute instructions for what is to be done and how, and checking up frequently with criticisms for every departure from your formulas, you will be disappointed that your youngsters do not take more responsibility. Too often they do not take responsibility because responsibility is not offered to them. When your children have the feeling that they are working with you on common tasks of their life together, they can and do assume responsibility as readily as do adults.

∞
Know your teenager's friends
In past years there have been changes in the relationship between people. The trend has been increasingly toward more informality, more easily expressed interest, and more spontaneous expression of affection. Young people rarely think of themselves as free in their relations with others. All around them are many people behaving in a variety of ways. The modern high school exposes every youth to many patterns of behavior that are new to him. Ruling groups make some types of behavior seem "smart," and those that struggle to belong follow along. They try to appear as sophisticated as the next one. This makes for a considerable amount of faking to cover the uncertainty and confusion just below the surface.

Today young people too often receive guidance that is too little and too late and must react impulsively to demands and pressures for which they are quite unprepared. The example of a happy, unfrustrated marriage, with frank discussion of the emotional and physical aspects of sex, and, above all, an example of truly Christian virtue, is the most useful contribution that you can give your children in this field.

Hence, it is important that you insist on meeting your children's friends and learn something about their background and reputation. Do not object to your children's boyfriends or girlfriends just because you happen to dislike them, even though there are no valid objections apart from your dislike.

Instill in your children's hearts, from early years, a knowledge of the difficulties and dangers connected with mixed marriages, and try to make them want to date and marry only a person of their own Faith.

Some parents permit their children to "go steady" at fifteen, fourteen, and even twelve. The formation of puppy-love affairs is one of the most dangerous and harmful things that parents can permit. First, adolescents, just awakening to the meaning of passion in themselves, and surrounded by many unprincipled and undirected adolescents who believe that passions are there to be exploited, will be in great danger of falling into sin. Such sins seldom start without continuing, because they engender habits that become stronger with the years while the character grows weaker. The second danger is that all the money, interest, and energy spent on the education of the adolescents will be wasted if they squander their opportunities and divide their attention by concentrating on company-keeping and premature courtship.

Do not permit or encourage "steady" dating for your children when there is no chance of their marrying within a reasonable period of time (about a year), and when they could only run into dangers against chastity and neglect the important years of their education. If your children find it difficult to understand why you strictly adhere to this principle, you can offset this difficulty, first, by earning a loyalty from your children through close association, self-sacrifice, and understanding, which will make them obey you against the whole world, if necessary; and second, by your earnest effort to fill so completely your children's lives with interests and hobbies that they will not be affected by the absence of dates.

∞

Strive for mutual confidence and understanding
between you and your teenagers

Be determined to protect your children from the moral disintegration of youth today. That will never be accomplished simply by a hard, dictatorial, unyielding attitude toward the pastimes of youth. Young people are not saved from sin by being locked up in a home, thundered at if they want to go to a dance, a show, or a party, or suspected of evil every time they spend an evening outside their home.

It is far better to earn their confidence, to instruct them about dangers, and to trust them as having some sense of responsibility themselves. It is far better to bend down to their level, to show them a good time of your own accord once in a while, to prove how much you want them to be happy, and then to use the confidence thus gained to convince them of the evils that endanger their lives.

Getting through to your teenagers across the barrier of age is often difficult, but is important for mutual understanding of common problems. As a parent, you must be willing to see your children as individuals in their own right. Your children must be able to view you as a real person, as well as a parent. Mutual respect and genuine affection, based on sound Catholic principles, are needed for understanding each other.

∽

Chapter Twenty-One

Foster love in your home

Two things in particular must be nurtured in the home: love and self-sacrifice. Sincere parental love makes the child home-centered and gives security, purpose, and direction to young lives. Self-sacrifice, demanded by discipline, remains the basis of order in the home. Firm parental discipline frees a child from his own confusion. It places the parents in their rightful place in the home. It sets the rules of family life and teaches respect for authority. If a child learns obedience early in life, he will extend that obedience to his teachers, and to wider authority as he matures.

As a parent, you stand in God's place in the home, and in such a position you have God's authority in training your children. Do not surrender that authority.

What a child needs more than anything else is to belong to two devoted, God-fearing parents who work together to bring about his eternal salvation. He wants a cheerful home where there is love, goodness, and generosity of heart. He needs the security of knowing his mother and father consider him a precious gift from God. He needs the faith that sustains a family whose members pray together and speak confidently of God watching over them. He needs parents strong enough to say, "This is right," or, "That is wrong," no matter what other people around them may be saying. He needs to share his parents' time and thoughts often enough and intimately enough to feel the blessed closeness that makes them a family living to love and serve God.

∞

Eight Beatitudes for the Home

Blessed is the home
where the father, mother, and children
love God sincerely and keep His commandments faithfully,
go to Confession regularly, receive Holy Communion frequently,
and pray much; for the Lord abides in such a home.

∞

Blessed is the home in which Sundays and holy days
are properly observed, for the members will one day
meet again at the festival of Heaven.

∞

Blessed is the home that no one leaves
to go to sinful amusements,
for in it the joy of Christ shall reign.

∞

Blessed is the home where unkind speech does not enter,
nor cursing, nor bad literature, nor intemperance,
for on that home will be heaped the blessings of peace.

∽

*Blessed is the home where father and mother are conscious
of the sacred dignity of bringing children into the world and
educating them in the service of God, where they faithfully fulfill
the obligations they have toward each other and their children,
and detest the sins sometimes committed in the married state,
for they will merit the favor and abundant blessings of God.*

∽

*Blessed is the home to which a priest is called to attend the sick,
for their illness will have its consolation and death will be happy.*

∽

*Blessed is the home where Christian doctrine is properly
appreciated and learned from the Catechism and good books,
for in that home, the Faith will be kept firm and active.*

∽

*Blessed is the home where the parents find their joy in children
who are dutiful and obedient, and where the children find
in their parents the example of the fear and love of God,
for that home will be the abode of just people,
the haven of virtues, and the ark of salvation.*

∽

*Where there is faith, there is love.
Where there is love, there is peace.
Where there is peace, there is God.
Where there is God, there is Heaven.*

Lawrence G. Lovasik

Biographical Note

∞

Lawrence G. Lovasik
(1913-1986)

"Life is short, and we must all give account of it on the Day of Judgment," said Fr. Lawrence Lovasik. "I am in earnest about using the time allotted to me by God on this earth to the best advantage in carrying out the ideal of my life — to make God more known and loved through my writings."[51]

The oldest of eight children, Lawrence Lovasik was born of Slovak parents in the steel-industry town of Tarentum, Pennsylvania. He was accepted into the Sacred Heart Mission Seminary in Girard, Pennsylvania, at the age of twelve and, after thirteen years of study and training, was ordained to the priesthood at St. Mary's Mission Seminary in Techny, Illinois, in 1938. Fr. Lovasik studied further at Rome's Gregorian Papal University, spent three years as a teacher and prefect of seminarians, and went on to do missionary work in America's coal and steel regions. In 1955, he founded the Sisters of the Divine Spirit, an American religious congregation of home

---

[51] Walter Romig, *The Book of Catholic Authors*, 5th ser. (Grosse Pointe, Michigan: Walter Romig and Company, 1943), 181.

and foreign missionaries whose services included teaching in schools and in catechetical classes, visiting homes, and assisting in social work.

Fr. Lovasik devoted much of his time to giving missions and retreats. These experiences and that of his earlier missionary work acquainted him with the spiritual needs, personal and family problems, and individual plans and longings of God's people, and he yearned to help them. Christ's exhortation to His first priests — "Go, and make disciples of all nations"[52] — was his inspiration. "I wanted to reach the hearts of people," he said, "but my voice could be heard only by those to whom I was able to preach."[53] Writing, he found, was his way to preach God's love and truth to the many, and it was his personal love for Christ, for the Blessed Mother, and for all immortal souls that drove him to dedicate himself to this talent.

Prayer and the Holy Eucharist are the emphases of many of the several books and more than fifty pamphlets that Fr. Lovasik wrote. His style is simple, sincere, and highly practical. He combines his vision of the transforming power of holiness and his compassionate understanding of man's desires and weaknesses to offer sound spiritual direction that motivates and inspires his readers, leads them step by step toward holiness, warns them against spiritual and temporal pitfalls, and guides them back to the right path when they go astray. Fr. Lovasik's wisdom not only reveals the often overlooked strength of holiness, but also continues to make real his life's ideal — to make God more known and loved.

[52] Matt. 28:19.
[53] Romig, *The Book of Catholic Authors*, 180.

Sophia Institute

Sophia Institute is a nonprofit institution that seeks to nurture the spiritual, moral, and cultural life of souls and to spread the Gospel of Christ in conformity with the authentic teachings of the Roman Catholic Church.

Sophia Institute Press fulfills this mission by offering translations, reprints, and new publications that afford readers a rich source of the enduring wisdom of mankind.

Sophia Institute also operates two popular online Catholic resources: CrisisMagazine.com and CatholicExchange.com.

Crisis Magazine provides insightful cultural analysis that arms readers with the arguments necessary for navigating the ideological and theological minefields of the day. *Catholic Exchange* provides world news from a Catholic perspective as well as daily devotionals and articles that will help you to grow in holiness and live a life consistent with the teachings of the Church.

In 2013, Sophia Institute launched Sophia Institute for Teachers to renew and rebuild Catholic culture through service to Catholic education. With the goal of nurturing the spiritual, moral, and cultural life of souls, and an abiding respect for the role and work of teachers, we strive to provide materials and programs that are at once enlightening to the mind and ennobling to the heart; faithful and complete, as well as useful and practical.

Sophia Institute gratefully recognizes the Solidarity Association for preserving and encouraging the growth of our apostolate over the course of many years. Without their generous and timely support, this book would not be in your hands.

www.SophiaInstitute.com
www.CatholicExchange.com
www.CrisisMagazine.com
www.SophiaInstituteforTeachers.org